Table of Contents

Parenting a Preschooler – A Long Term Journey   7

PART 1   **BUILDING CONFIDENCE AND ENCOURAGING**   15
             LEARNING

Step 1   Becoming a Responsive Parent   17
Step 2   The Power of Play   26
Step 3   Helping Children Learn Through
           Play and Creative Activities   38
Step 4   The Importance of Encouragement and Praise   51
Step 5   Teaching Children New Tasks and Routines   62

PART 2   **TEACHING CHILDREN TO BEHAVE WELL**   73

Step 6   Responding to Misbehaviour   75
Step 7   The Power of Attention   83
Step 8   Setting Rules with Children   93
Step 9   Assertive Parenting – Following Through
           on Rules   101
Step 10   Using Rewards to Teach Children to
           Behave Well   111

This book is dedicated to the parents and children we worked with
in the making of the Parents Plus Early Years Programme.
We remain inspired and grateful for their generosity.

Parenting a Preschooler — A Long Term Journey

BECOMING A PARENT OF A TODDLER

As your child grows up and changes from being a baby to becoming a more independent toddler, this new stage is marked by change. Children discover speech and begin to communicate in a meaningful way; they learn to walk and become increasingly mobile, they are more aware of the world and themselves in it. Above all, young toddlers begin to discover their own independent will; they realise that they have their own wishes and preferences (often very different than those of their parents!). These changes can bring lots of joys to parents, such as the pleasure of talking to and listening to your child as they use new words and come up with their own ideas, or the pleasure of watching them explore the world and make their own decisions, or the delight in seeing them learn and try out new experiences.

The arrival of a toddler, however, also brings new challenges to parents such as dealing with the 'battle of wills' with young children who want to be in control or the temper tantrums that arise as toddlers seek to get their own way or deal with frustration. The toddler stage of development can also bring about new worries and concerns for parents. You can become increasingly aware of comparisons between your child and other children and worry about whether or not they are developing normally or learning things as quickly as their peers are. For parents of children with special needs it can be a challenging time as these needs can be heightened and you wonder how best to respond to help your child.

WHO THIS BOOK IS FOR?

This book is for all parents of toddlers and preschool children who are looking for ways to help their children reach their full potential and to grow up to be confident and secure as well-adjusted adults. In particular, the book aims to help parents answer questions such as:

- What is the best way to develop a good relationship with my child?
- How can I improve his/her attention and concentration?
- How can I help my child improve his/her understanding and learning?
- How can I help my child develop more language?
- What is the best way to help my child be more cooperative and to do more of what I say?

- What is the best way to manage tantrums and other behaviour problems?
- What is the best way to teach my child?

The ideas in this book are derived from a special course – the Parents Plus Early Years Programme (PPEY) – which was developed in the Department of Child and Family Psychiatry in the Mater Hospital in Dublin. The PPEY is designed to empower parents to find their own solutions to parenting problems and to help them find suitable ways of helping their children develop and learn to the best of their ability. Like the ideas in this book, the focus of the PPEY is on how parents interact with their children – when parents respond differently to their children, they help their children behave differently in turn. By becoming aware of and sensitive to how you interact and communicate with your children, you can find ways to reduce behavioural problems, help them learn to the best of their ability and help them feel confident and secure. In addition, such sensitive child-centred communication is the best way to get the most out of children and to enjoy being their parent.

CHILDREN WITH SPECIAL NEEDS

The Parents Plus Early Years Programme was developed to be beneficial to both parents of children who are developing normally and children with special needs. As a result the principles of this book are relevant to the concerns of parents dealing with the normal ups and downs of raising a pre-schooler and parents who are dealing with the specific challenges of raising a child with special needs such as:

- delays in learning and language development.
- poor attention, over-activity or ADHD (Attention Deficit Hyperactive Disorder).

- specific behavioural problems.
- mild autistic type difficulties.

Though parents of children with special needs may face specific challenges, the principles in this book will complement any professional or educational help you are already receiving and provide some ideas on how to make progress. It is important to note that while the principles are not a replacement for seeking appropriate professional advice and support in relation to your children, they will provide you with ideas on making progress.

HOW TO USE THIS BOOK

This book is designed to be read either straight through from beginning to end or to be dipped in and out of depending on a specific question. This book is divided into two sections:

1) Building Confidence and Encouraging Learning.
2) Teaching Children to Behave Well.

Part 1 outlines a set of ideas on how you can use play and everyday interaction with children as opportunities to connect with and enjoy their company as well as helping them learn and develop at their own pace. This section also describes how you can teach young children new tasks and routines in a child-centred way and is relevant to all parents, especially those who are facing developmental concerns in their children. The positive principles contained in Part 1 also form the basis to solving behavioural problems in Part 2.

Part 2 considers the challenge of misbehaviour in young children, reframing this as the long term project of teaching children how to behave well as they grow up. This section provides a number of strategies that are generally useful in dealing with misbehaviour and the aim is to provide parents with a 'tool-kit' of options that they can draw upon in the face of problems.

While the ideas in the book have proved useful to most families, none apply in every situation or in all contexts. Each parent, each child and each family is different, and it is the parents who know their children and their families best. Rather than giving you ready-made solutions, the aim of this book is to encourage you to pause and reflect about your parenting methods and to discover what works best for you with your children. We invite you to adapt the ideas and suggestions provided in this book to your own unique family situation.

BE ENCOURAGING TOWARDS YOURSELF AS A PARENT

Probably the most important principle that we emphasise in this book is the principle of encouragement – we invite you to go out of your way to encourage and notice your children's strengths and to praise them for what they are doing right. We argue that this is not only the best way to help your children learn and develop, it also allows you as a parent to get the most out of any interaction with them. In addition, encouragement is also the best way to build a positive relationship with your children and is by far a much more enjoyable (and effective) way to parent than being critical or confrontational.

While many parents accept this encouraging stance towards their children, they can be very negative and undermining towards themselves. Too often parents give themselves a hard

I ENCOURAGE YOU TO SPEND MORE TIME ENCOURAGING YOURSELF AS A PARENT!

time, criticising their own behaviour and putting themselves down. Too often they focus on what they do wrong in every situation, thinking, 'I wish I hadn't lost my patience like that' or 'I should have more time for my children'. Similarly, parents in couple relationships can relate negatively to each other, focusing on what the other has done wrong: 'I don't like the way you interrupted me when I was talking to the kids' or 'You shouldn't have lost your temper'.

In this book, we encourage you to adopt not only an encouraging stance towards your children, but also towards yourselves as parents. We encourage you to build on your strengths and start looking for what you and your partner are doing right as parents. Be on the lookout for the small steps of improvement you make each day, the times you manage successfully. Begin to notice what you like about yourself as a parent. Don't be afraid to praise yourself: 'I'm pleased at how I was firm in that instance' or 'I'm glad that I at least tried my best'. Equally, if you are part of a couple, be on the lookout for examples of behaviour you like in your partner: 'Thanks for supporting me with Peter like that' or 'I'm really pleased that you came home early and we had some time to ourselves'.

It is in your children's interests that you identify your own strengths and successes. Children learn a powerful lesson from you when you model self-encouragement. They learn how to be confident and successful and how to relate positively to other people.

START WITH CARING FOR YOURSELF AS A PARENT

While in this parenting book we talk about the needs of preschool children and what parents should do to care for them, we do not want you to forget about your own needs as parents or as individual people. Unfortunately, many parents we meet are stressed and over-tired. They have become so focused on their children's needs and problems and put so much energy into this that there is little time and attention for themselves. Sadly, while their intentions are good, the long-term results are bad for themselves and their children. If you are over-tired and stressed, you can no longer be there for your children; you can even become negative, inconsistent and resentful in your parenting.

While most of this book is about the importance of providing positive attention and care to children, whether this is by setting time aside to play with them or by being positive and encouraging or by taking time to teach them, it is equally crucial, however, that you treat yourself in the same way! The first suggestion we give to stressed parents is that they try to turn some of the care and attention that they have lavished on their children towards themselves. We suggest that they redirect some of the energy and instead think about prioritising their own needs and wants – whether this is ensuring they get a break each day, keeping in touch with friends, keeping fit and eating well or whatever works in each particular case.

The irony is that such a switch to self-care often benefits your children as much as yourself. When your own needs for care, comfort and fulfilment are met, you are freed up to attend fully to the parenting role. Children need cared-for parents as much as they need parents to care for them. The best way to help your children grow up to be confident people with high self-esteem is for you as their parent to model this – that is, to take steps to value, love and prioritise yourself.

A NOTE ON LANGUAGE

Throughout this book, in order to avoid the cumbersome 'he/she' structure, we alternate between the pronouns 'he' and 'she' when referring to individual children and the plural 'they' when referring to children or parents collectively.

Part 1

Building Confidence and

Encouraging Learning

STEP 1

BECOMING A RESPONSIVE PARENT

Three-year-old James was very active and energetic. His mother used to spend the whole day 'running after him' and she could be really worn out by the end of day. It became really hard for her to manage. She wondered how she could get him to slow down.

Four-year-old Tara can be really difficult in the mornings. She refuses to get up and resists getting dressed. Her parents, who are in a rush to get her to preschool so they can go to work, find this really frustrating and the mornings can set a bad atmosphere for the whole day.

BECOMING A RESPONSIVE PARENT

Being a parent involves strong feelings that cause us to react in certain ways. This is especially the case when we face the daily challenges and problems of parenting. Sometimes our immediate reactions are helpful, for example, when we naturally respond to soothe a child who is crying. But other times they can be unhelpful, for example, if we react by 'flying off the handle' or if we react passively and take no action at all. Reactions are simply habits (good or bad) that we have developed over the years, perhaps a repetition of how we were treated by our own parents in the past. The trouble with reactions is that we don't choose them, and in fact they choose us. Whether it is 'flying off the handle' or 'giving the silent treatment', reactions can control us and we can become stuck repeating them over and over again and reacting the same way to the same problem.

In this book we invite you to become a responsive parent, which is the opposite of a reactive parent. Responsive parents take time to consider how best to respond to their child or to a specific situation. Responsive parents are both aware of their own feelings and needs and tuned into the needs and feelings of their children. Responsive parents *adapt* how they respond to their children, depending on their child's needs and the situation in question. Being responsive instead of reactive, allows us to choose our response and gives us the basis from which we can solve problems. Being a responsive parent involves the following stages:

1 Pausing.
2 Tuning into your child.
3 Tuning into yourself.
4 Choosing your response.

MUM! I'M WAKING DADDY UP EARLY SO HE CAN BE A RESPONSIVE PARENT- BUT HE DOESN'T SEEM TO WANT TO RESPOND!

PAUSING

A central feature of a being a responsive parent is being able to pause. Rather than reacting, you are able to step back and think: 'What way do I want to respond now as a parent?' or 'What is the best way to deal with this problem?' or 'What is the right way to respond to my child now?' Such a pause gives you the chance to think how you want to respond to whatever situation you are dealing with. If you are concerned about your child's lack of concentration, for instance, you can ask yourself, 'How can I play with my child in a way that will improve his concentration?' or if you are worried about your child's misbehaviour, you can ask, 'How can I teach my child in a positive way to behave well?'

TUNING INTO YOUR CHILD

As a responsive parent you are able to appreciate your child's point of view. You are able to step into your child's shoes and see the world as she sees it. Whether this is appreciating how your two-year-old daughter loves playdough or how she's becoming frustrated late at night, or appreciating how your four-year-old son likes physical games and hates any changes in routine, the principle is the same – you empathise with and understand how your child feels and thinks. It is a bit like tuning into a radio station; if you adjust how you listen and make an effort to get on your child's wavelength you begin to get the signal loud and clear!

Being able to 'tune into your child' forms the basis of a good parent-child relationship. It helps your children feel attached and close to you, because they sense that you understand them, and it makes parenting enjoyable and fun as you feel close and connected to them.

Tuning into your children is also the best way to manage childhood difficulties and to help your children if they have special needs. In their first years of life, young children are developing in many ways, learning lots of new and complex skills. Their best and most important teachers are their parents. Being on your child's wavelength makes it easier to help them develop and learn. You can't help a child learn unless you tune in first and know exactly where he is coming from. For example, when helping children learn new language, speech and language therapists first spend a lot of time joining with children in play and in following their lead, before introducing new words and ideas which are connected to what the child is doing. Equally, being a responsive parent and tuning into children forms the basis for solving specific behavioural problems (as we shall see in more detail in Part 2 of the book).

THE BEST WAY TO TUNE IN

It is important to tune into your child throughout the day. When dressing your child in the morning, take a moment to see how he is feeling and thinking. This way you can make the experience of getting dressed run more smoothly and even make it enjoyable. When doing chores try and involve your child a little, for example, when sweeping the floor let your child hold the dustpan and then you can work together in each other's company.

It is also a good idea to set aside a regular playtime with your child when you can tune into and connect with one another and most importantly enjoy each other's company. In the next section, we describe in more detail the skills of child-centred play and communication, but for the moment here are some ideas to get you started.

Watch and Listen

Rather than assuming you know, take a little time to watch and observe your child closely to see what he is interested in at any given time. How he is feeling... Happy? Bored? Interested? Frustrated?

Wait

Rather than jumping in with your own plans, be prepared to wait and let your child come up with his own ideas, so you can respond to him rather than direct him. Waiting and watching is especially important for children who have difficulty concentrating and who need more time to articulate their own ideas.

Get down to your child's level

Make sure you get down to your child's eye level so that you can see his face and he can see yours. This is the best position for you to see what is going on from his perspective and to appreciate what the world looks like from his angle.

Go at your child's pace

Young children always play at a slower rate than adults. They like to repeat the same actions and to play with things over and over again. It is easy as an adult to get bored and to want to move on to other games. However, in order to tune into a small child's mentality, we have to make sure we slow down to his pace. This is especially the case with a child who has concentration problems, or delayed development.

Taking time to tune into your child and to follow his or her ideas like this does not come naturally to many parents, but it will pay dividends in building confidence and communication, and the play will be more relaxed and enjoyable.

TUNING INTO YOURSELF AS A PARENT

As well as tuning into your children, it is important to tune in to yourself as a parent. Responsive parents are sensitive to and aware of their own thoughts and feelings as well as those of their children. You might notice that you are feeling frustrated, for instance, and become aware that if you tackle your child now on his bad behaviour you are likely to become angry. As a result, you may decide to take a break for a moment and deal with the problem later when you feel calmer. Or in another situation, you might notice that you are feeling positive and upbeat, and realise that this is a good time to organise a spontaneous trip for you and your children which you can all enjoy. Learning to 'tune into' yourself and understand your moods and needs is also important in solving problems. Consider the example of the father below:

> Joe worked in a high-powered job that made great demands on him. When he came home to his wife and children, he would frequently be preoccupied and stressed. Often he would be grumpy and snap angrily at his children over minor things. He used to collapse in front of the TV and not even have time to play with them. When he had time away, Joe began to reflect on how out-of-balance his life had become. He realised that his family and children were more important than his work and wanted to be more present for them. As a result he began to change his working hours in order to get home earlier. A useful routine he found was to take a fifteen-minute walk through the park before he went home. During this time to himself, he would unwind and let go the stress of the day. He would prepare himself to arrive home, present and attentive to his children who would want his attention.

As the example above suggests, being a responsive caring parent means taking care of your own needs as well as your children's. In the long-term this self-care is best for our children as they need their parents to be positive, attentive and upbeat (rather than tired or irritable). Children need cared-for parents as much as they need parents to care for them.

CHOOSING YOUR RESPONSE

By pausing and tuning into children and yourself, you will allow for space so that you can choose how you want to respond. It gives you the awareness of what is best for you and your children. Consider the following examples:

Not being able to concentrate

> My three-year-old son is very hyperactive and I am always on the go trying to keep up with him. One of the things I always worried about was his concentration. He would flit from toy to toy and never really learn. I would try hard to keep him on task and he would resist this. When I got some support I was able to realise how best to help him. Part of the reason he was so inattentive was that there was always too much going on around him so I changed this. I made sure the TV was off and that there was only one toy or activity available at a time. I also slowed down myself and took time to notice what he wanted to do. This made a big difference in helping him concentrate. The situation is not perfect but at least I can make progress.

The morning rush

My four-year-old girl used to be really difficult in the mornings. She would be really slow and resist every step to get dressed and ready. It used to really drive me mad because I was rushing to take her to preschool and to get to work. When I took time to think about the problem, I realised that it was probably simply due to the fact that she was really tired and needed more time in the morning. Much of the rush we were under could be avoided. So I changed our routine, and we went to bed earlier giving more time in the morning. I found the time to enjoy having breakfast with her and to take more time with the dressing. I also changed my work routine and stopped scheduling early morning appointments, so that if necessary I could take a little more time over breakfast.

Visiting nightmare

My six-year-old boy used to play up when we were visiting relatives. Invariably he would be really cranky or rude with the adults and sometimes he would get into a fight with his cousins. It would sour the whole visit for us as a family. However, when I took time to notice what was going on for him during the visits I realised that he wasn't just 'being naughty' but rather he was very anxious and awkward when visiting. He found it hard to socialise with the other kids (who were older than him) and this caused the problems. I realised that he needed lots of preparation and support to get through it. Thinking about him as an anxious rather than a difficult child made me more sensitive and more able to help him.

TIPS FOR GOING FORWARD

1 Take some time to 'tune into' your children over the next few days. Spend time watching what they are interested in, listening to how they are feeling and being in their company.
2 Think of a problem or ongoing situation that you would like to improve in your family.
3 Take a moment to 'tune into' the situation – what is going on for your children and yourself that gives rise to the problem?
4 Choose a new way of responding to the situation that might work better.

STEP 2

THE POWER OF PLAY

I was always in a rush as a parent and there was never any time for play or fun. There was so much to be done with getting the children washed, fed and dressed, keeping the house clean and trying to hold down a job. This was putting great stress on myself and the kids. Learning to slow down and be much more 'playful' has made a huge difference to my family. Basically, I've learnt to reprioritise – when it is a choice between cleaning the house and taking time to listen to or play with my kids, I try to choose play these days. We all benefit!

THE VALUE OF PLAYTIME

In our busy world, it is easy to see play as 'unserious' or something unimportant. Certainly, play is seen as something that children are left to get on with while the parents do more important adult things. However, this is far from the truth: play is enormously important for children. Through play children not only have fun, they also learn new skills and abilities, express feelings and learn how to get along with other children. Play between parents and children is particularly valuable as children don't automatically know how to play and need the support of a parent to help them get the most out of it. Parent–child play provides many benefits:

- Playtime can be a relaxing and enjoyable experience for parents as well as for children.
- Parent–child play promotes children's physical, intellectual, emotional and social development.

- Playtime brings parent and child closer emotionally.
- Child-centred play allows children to take the lead, make decisions and become more confident.
- Child-centred play is the best way to stimulate a child's development and imagination as well as helping her learn new skills and to practise new tasks.
- Play helps children learn how to communicate and learn new language.
- By playing with their children, parents can help them concentrate and spend more time at activities.
- Regular positive parent–child play forms the basis for solving many childhood problems, such as tantrums or defiant behaviour.

Indeed we can't emphasise enough the importance of parent–child play, both in the normal course of a child's development and when dealing with specific problems.

BEING PLAYFUL AND CHILD-CENTRED IN EVERYDAY ACTIVITIES

Playing with children and being child-centred is something you can do throughout the day and not just during a specific 'play time'. Make the most of household chores and tasks by ensuring your child can get involved in a playful way. For example, when doing the gardening why not take an extra bit of time to get your children involved. You could use the activity as an opportunity to connect with and enjoy your children's company and to teach them lots of new language. Even chores and routine activities can be transformed if you take a little more time to be child-centred. Instead of rushing when dressing your children in the morning, take time to go at their pace and use the time as an opportunity to interact and listen to them. Being child-centred in everyday activities is the best way to enjoy their company, teach them new things and to develop a good relationship.

> When I used to make the dinner in the evening I was in a rush and my little three-year-old was always in the way getting under my feet. I was always trying to shoo her away so I could get on with the dinner. She would often resist and the whole situation could be quite pressured. But then I realised that she only wanted to be with me and be involved in the dinner. I changed my routine so I had a little more time to involve her as I worked. If I was washing vegetables I would allow her to wash some too. She was delighted to get involved and all along we were chatting and talking. Though it took a little longer, it was much more enjoyable and definitely less pressured.

FINDING TIME TO PLAY

As well as 'being playful' and getting the most out of everyday situations and interaction, it is very useful to set aside a special time each day to play with your children. In a busy parent's schedule, this may need to be planned in advance and prioritised as something important and not to be missed. Playtime doesn't have to be long to be worthwhile and enjoyable. With young children (up to six years of age) short daily play sessions of fifteen minutes can make a real difference. It can be useful to build a routine around playtime. Maybe you set aside fifteen minutes just after dinner or just before bedtime. After a while you will find that both you and your child will look forward to this special time together.

Though you can organise times to play with two or more of your children, it is also important to find time to play with your child individually. While this can put extra demands on parents with larger families, there is no substitute for one-on-one time with a child, in terms of getting to know him deeply and building an enduring bond with him. Even if it means slightly shorter or less frequent special times, it is still best to have quality one-on-one time with your child. This is the foundation of good family life, and happy healthy relationships.

> It was really helpful for me to build a regular playtime into my routine with my four-year-old. As part of her bedtime routine we would have ten minutes play time when she could choose the game or toys. We would follow this by getting ready for bed and a quiet story just before sleep. This regular time became important to us both and she would often chat and open up to me during this time.

THE BEST WAY TO PLAY

Play is not something automatic that children know how to do. They need to learn and develop play skills over time. Equally, parents don't automatically know how to play with their children, but once again it is something that can be learnt. Having fun through trial and error is usually the best way! Below we list some of the principles of child-centred play that can be very effective with young children. This form of child-centred play is not only fun, it has also been researched as a very effective way of promoting children's development and communication. By adopting child-centred play and interaction you maximise your child's learning capacity. (This will be explored in more detail in the next chapter.)

Choose interactive, imaginative activities

The best toys and play materials are those that stimulate a child's imagination and creativity. They don't have to be expensive, educational toys. We all see children who turn away from the expensive toy to transform the box and wrapper into an imaginative castle!

The best toys allow children to be active and creative rather than passive and non-communicative (as with television viewing). Good toys facilitate communication and talking between parent and child. It is important to choose toys that match a child's age and ability level as well as their personality and interests. Below are some suggestions for play and special time to which you can add your own ideas:

- playdough, plasticine
- blocks/Lego (any building or construction kits)
- dolls/figures/puppets/toy animals
- tea-set, tool-set

- farmhouse, doll's house
- soft toys
- dress up box
- paints, crayons, colours
- jigsaws, shapesorters (remember to choose these appropriate to your child's age level)

Get down to your child's level

Play goes best when you get down to your child's level to ensure you are facing each other and can make eye contact easily, making it very easy for you to communicate. This usually means getting down on the floor with your child, or sitting on a small chair with him at a table or having him sit on your lap. When playing it is important to have a friendly interested expression on your face. With very young children much of the communication will be non-verbal; they will look to the expression on your face for affirmation and encouragement.

Following your child's lead

In child-centred play, children should be encouraged to take charge and make most of the decisions. Parents should 'tune into' their children and let them lead the play. Children have many other areas in life where parents are in charge, so playtime is their chance to try out decision-making and to develop confidence. Parents can sit back and follow the child's lead, valuing and affirming his imagination and initiative. With young children this simply means letting the child choose the game or activity and how to play it, while being there to notice value and affirm this.

Following your children's lead in this way keeps them interested and supported in the play, promotes their learning and is a good way to build their confidence. While there are situations when parents should introduce new ideas and suggestions to the play as a way of helping children learn (and these will be explored in the next chapter), the starting point in teaching is always to first follow the child's lead.

Imitating sounds and actions

As well as using verbal language, it is very important that we back up our words with gestures, sounds and actions to make sure our child feels understood. This is especially important for those who have little language. Children learn more easily from what we show them than what we tell them. In child-centred play, as well as repeating the words a child makes, it is also useful to repeat his sounds and actions. If your child bangs on a drum, for example, you can repeat the action and watch for his response. If he smiles with glee and claps his hands when the tower falls you match his smile and clap with him. If he begins to hum a tune, maybe you can hum along too. Imitating sounds and actions in this way not only helps your child feel understood, but it gives you an opportunity to join in.

Descriptive Commenting

When adults play with children there is a tendency to ask a lot of questions, such as 'What are you doing now?' or 'Are you building a castle?'. While some questions are a good idea, too many can put a child under pressure and close down communication. As an alternative to questions, it is a good idea to make comments when playing with children, for example, 'Oh, I see you are building a castle' or 'Oh, you picked a green block'. Comments are an excellent way of joining in with children and staying in tune with them. They let the child know you are interested in what they are doing without pressurising them. There are a number of different ways to make comments, which we list below:

Putting words on OBJECTS
By putting words on the items that your child is using, you provide him with a great opportunity to learn new words and their meaning. For example:

> 'It's a *helicopter*.'
> 'That's called a *hippo*.'

It can also be useful to say what you think your child is trying to express; if your child points at teddy saying, 'That', you say, 'That's *Teddy*', emphasising the new word as you say it.

Putting words on ACTIONS:
By commenting on what your child is doing, you let him know that you are noticing all his efforts and the good things he does. This will help build his confidence. Describing what is happening will also help your child focus on the task at hand and can help keep the activity going. By adding some specific praise, you encourage your child further. For example:

Your child's actions

> 'You're *pushing* the button; that's great.'
> 'I see you're *looking* out the window.'
> 'Wow! You've *taken* all the pieces out.'

Your own actions
You can also comment on your own actions to help your child learn new words and to understand routines. Naming your own actions not only helps your child understand what is happening, it also helps include you in his world. For example:

> 'I'm *watching* you eat your dinner.'
> 'I'm *cleaning* the floor now and then I will *sit* and *play* with you.'

Putting words on FEELINGS:
By naming how your child is feeling, you help her feel understood and provide her with a word to express herself in a positive way. Expressing empathy with your child like this is powerful in building her emotional security and sense of herself. Parents may feel wary of naming their children's negative feelings fearing that this may focus too much attention on the situation. However, the opposite is true in that when children feel understood emotionally, they learn to deal with their feelings and move on.

Your child's feelings

> 'I know you're *sad* because...'
> 'You're *disappointed*...'
> 'You *like* that!'
> 'You *want to go* out now but...'

Your own feelings

> 'I'm *sad* because...'
> 'I'm *tired* from working so hard. I think I'll sit down now.'

Encourage Children in Play

It's easy to fall into the trap of correcting children when they play. Out of a desire to teach children, parents can find themselves being critical, saying, 'Oh, that doesn't go there' or 'It should be done like this'. We suggest that for special playtime, you go out of your way to encourage children, looking for things they are doing right and showing great interest in their activities. You can use lots of positive comments such as:

'I like that colour you picked.'

'It was a good idea to turn it around that way.'

'You're really trying hard to get this house made.'

Essentially it is about being a good audience to children in their play, taking a great interest in what they are doing, getting down to their level, providing lots of eye contact and good body language. Using encouraging statements and kind comments helps children continue in their play and promotes a rewarding experience for both parent and child.

Listening in Play

Essentially, what we are talking about is listening. The skills of child-centred play boil down to listening to them. By naming what they are doing, imitating their actions and gestures, and repeating what they have said, you show that you have understood them.

Being able to listen is seen as the essence of good communication. We can use the letters of the word LISTEN to remind us of the key qualities of child-centred communication:

> **L** ook at your child's interest or idea.
>
> **I** mitate what he is doing to show him you notice.
>
> **S** it at his level so that you can see each other's faces.
>
> **T** ell him what's happening by saying what he is doing and what you are doing.
>
> **E** njoy each other and let it show in your face and body language.
>
> **N** ame the feelings you both have at that moment.

PLAYING WITH CHILDREN TOGETHER

As well as setting one-on-one time aside to play with your child, it is useful to set up times when you can play with all your children together, or to join your child when he is playing with a friend. By taking time to join children in play, you can guide them in learning how to get on with one another as well as creating a shared fun-time between them. Such shared playtime and activities are great ways to bring families together.

All the principles of child-centered play apply equally well to playing with two or more children. The essential difference is that with two or more children your attention is divided as a parent. You have to make sure to switch your attention between your children making sure they get roughly the same amount of attention. In addition, it is useful to link the children to one another by using joint comments or praise. Consider the following steps to playing with two children:

1 Sit between the two children (or directly opposite them), so you can face each of them and can give them both attention easily.

2 Ensure both children have an activity that they want to do. Children at different ages or developmental levels may choose very different activities or may play with toys very differently.

3 Make sure to share attention frequently between the children, supporting them in their play and ensuring each of them gets lots of attention.

4 Use lots of commenting as with a single child, for example, 'Pete has the blue block, and Julie has the green block.'

5 Notice any times the children connect with one another and comment on this, 'Oh, David is looking at Jean's big tower' or 'You gave Pete a brick – that was kind' or ' You both like to play with the snake'. These comments help them notice and play with one another and can make a game go more smoothly.

I must say I used to find playing with my two-year-old a little bit repetitive. He would want to pile the same set of blocks over and over again and to be honest I found it boring at times. However, through attending a parenting course I began to see the value of play. It was an experience for me to slow down, and enter into my child's world and see play from his perspective. I saw how he was experimenting and learning as he piled the blocks over and over again. The big thing was becoming aware of his feelings – for him all this was still new and exciting. I realised how special it was for me to share in his discovery of the world and to really take part in his learning. Play became much more enjoyable.

TIPS FOR GOING FORWARD

1 Plan to be child-centred in a daily activity (getting dressed, eating dinner, for instance) and watch to see what happens.
2 Set up a regular playtime with your child (fifteen minutes a day can be sufficient) when you can give your child your full attention and let them lead the play.

STEP 3

HELPING CHILDREN LEARN THROUGH PLAY AND CREATIVE ACTIVITIES

Because I was worried that my child's rate of development was slow I used to try and teach him. I remember I used to ask him a lot of questions like 'what's this?' or 'what's that?' to test his knowledge, but he would rarely answer and would often close down. Looking back I realise this put him under even more pressure and wasn't helping. Through attending speech therapy, I became more child-centred in my approach, waiting for and encouraging any communication he made as well as using activities he was really interested in. Using this approach my son would communicate a lot more and he got a lot more out of my 'teaching sessions' with him.

Parents naturally want to help their children to learn and develop and to reach their full potential. In the last chapter we highlighted the importance of adopting a child-centred approach to playing and interacting with children and how this helps children learn at their own pace. In this chapter we expand on these child-centred skills to illustrate in more detail how they can be used to promote children's language and development.

EXPANDING CHILDREN'S LANGUAGE AND THINKING

The best way to help children learn new language and ideas is to add and build upon the language and ideas they have already.

First it is important to 'tune into' your children and to listen to and acknowledge the sounds, words and language that they already use. You can do this by copying their sounds and actions and repeating the words they use. To help your children develop even more language, it is then important to add some new ideas, elaborating on what they say and thus providing them with a new opportunity to learn. The following are different ways of giving your child new ideas in a way that will help them learn:

1 Describing your Child's Actions And Objects:

Your child is most likely to learn when you describe what she is interested in or what she is doing or about to do. As this information matches her own interest and focus she is more likely to absorb it and take it in because she hears the exact words that fit what she is doing, for example, 'You put the fireman up on the roof' or 'You gave the donkey grass'.

2 Describing your Own Actions

Using a phrase like, 'My horse is hungry, he's eating the grass' helps your child to notice you and to include you in the game. By saying, 'I'm going into the kitchen to make the dinner' your child understands what you are doing next (and realises that you're not just disappearing!).

3 Describing Feelings:

When you name your own feelings, for example, 'I love your funny clown – he makes me laugh,' and your child's feelings, 'Ah, you're sore, you hurt your finger', this helps your child to understand how he feels and how other people feel, and it gives him the words to express his own feelings.

4 Describing other things

Describing how something feels or what it looks like helps your child learn important concepts, for example, 'Your teddy feels soft. He has big shiny eyes.'

5 Interpreting

For children who don't have much language it is important to interpret their gestures and sounds, for example, if a child points to a broken car, the parent says, 'Yes, it's broken, the wheel fell off'. Your child is thus encouraged to communicate more when he feels understood.

6 Explaining

Your child understands what is going on in his world when you explain how things are linked, for example, 'Your sister is crying because she fell in a puddle and now she's all wet'.

7 Comparing

Comparing what your child is doing or seeing now to a previous experience, for example, 'That train is like your Thomas the Tank Engine'. This helps your child see how things and events are connected and encourages her to talk about her own experience.

8 Questions

Questions can encourage your child's thinking skills when they are used sparingly and are genuine and creative, or when you yourself don't know the answer. If a child puts a doll to bed, and the parent asks, 'Why is dolly in bed?' the answer could be 'Cause it's bedtime' or 'Cause she's sick'. This can lead the child to think of new ideas in the game and help the communication progress.

STAGES OF TEACHING

In simple terms you can follow the stages below as you teach your child and help them learn in a child-centred way which is more likely to be effective:

1 WAIT to let your child communicate first or come up with an idea or action.
2 ACKNOWLEDGE your child's idea or REPEAT what your child says ('It's a train').
3 Give them a NEW IDEA/WORD ('It's a *long* train').
4 WAIT to see how your child responds.

There are lots of different ways of expanding on your child's ideas. For example:

If your child says:	You could give an extra 'action' word:
'Car'	'You're *driving* the car.'
'Fish'	'Yes. The fish is *swimming*!'

You could say where the item is:
'The car is *under the bridge*.'
'The fish is *in the water*.'

You could describe the item:
'The car is *fast*.'
'It's a *big yellow* fish.'

You could describe a feeling:
'The boy is *sad* because…'
'The fish is *hungry*. He wants his dinner.'

The crucial thing is to make sure to go at your child's learning pace. Make sure to pause after you give a new idea (before adding another one) so your child has a chance to take in the information. Consider the simple example below:

Two-year-old Sam is playing with blocks. His dad is sitting down at his level, carefully watching him play. He sees Sam pick up a train:

> Sam: Choo choo.
> Dad: Yes, *train* says 'choo choo'.
> *(Sam pushes the train back and forth)*
> Dad: Sam is *driving* the train.
> Sam: Driving train.
> Dad: *(excitement in voice)* You are driving *a big train*... wow!
> Sam: *(matching Dad's excitement)* Yeah a *big* train.

In the above example, the father is not only engaged in enjoyable play with Sam he is also helping him learn language by naming what Sam is doing, repeating what he says, emphasising key words and by getting down to Sam's level. All these activities help maximise the connection between them and Sam's rate of learning. It is also important that the father has slowed down to Sam's pace. While it is easy to rush ahead of your children with new ideas, it is more helpful if you slow down and go at their pace.

The importance of repetition

In order to learn and remember new words and to understand their meaning, your child may need to hear the word many times in different contexts. For example:

> 'That's a *hippo*'...WAIT... 'The *hippo* is eating his dinner'...WAIT...'The *hippo* has a big mouth'... WAIT... 'I think this *hippo* is hungry!'

It is important to go slowly as you give new information and to wait between each sentence to give your child an opportunity to repeat the word(s) or add his own ideas.

> *My child was obsessed by trains, so much so that he would play with nothing else and would rarely talk about anything else. Anytime I tried to introduce another toy he would push it to one side. I was very worried that his play was so rigid that he wasn't learning and it was preventing him playing with other children.*
>
> *Things changed when instead of fighting his interest in trains, I joined with him and then used this interest to help him learn. I would listen to all his descriptions about trains and then use these as things to build upon. For example, we could explore how the wheels went round, or the different colours on the engine, or how to put the tracks together. Or when the train went on a journey we could make up a story about where he went and talk about the people he met. This new approach provided opportunities for lots of communication and learning. Aside from helping him communicate more, it allowed me to get much closer to him and to enjoy playing with him.*

SETTING UP OPPORTUNITIES TO PROMOTE LEARNING

Helping children learn is also about setting up great learning opportunities for them throughout the day, when you can interact with them in a child-centred way and help them learn and communicate. In particular, 1) Reading Books Together, 2) Using Music and Songs and 3) Creative Play Activities all provide great learning and play options for children.

1   Reading books together

Looking through books together can be an important learning and fun experience for you and your child for a number of reasons:

- Books and stories allow your child to develop new vocabulary and learn about things that are beyond their own experiences.
- Storybooks provide children with an opportunity to look at situations from a different point of view, and learn ideas about how to behave and respond to situations.
- Books help the child develop curiosity as she tries to anticipate what will happen next. Using books together regularly and pointing to pictures together helps the child learn the skills of focused attention.
- Books also provide a valuable way for parent and child to be close and to sit together.

Books for different stages

Your child's response to books and stories will change as she develops. The younger child may look at books only briefly and is more likely to be interested in picture books that refer to familiar routines and popular objects, naming items as they go. As they develop, children will begin to enjoy books that have an imaginative story as well as pictures. Generally children like to reread a favourite book several times. Children enjoy predicting what will happen next and will increasingly relate to and talk about the actions in the pictures and may ask many questions. Even children who are starting to recognise and read the text of stories will benefit from pictures to follow the meaning and to hold their attention.

The best way to use books

Looking at books together can be especially difficult for children who are very active. For reluctant readers it is helpful to incorporate book time into a daily routine, for example, looking at a book together before going to sleep at night, or on a daily bus journey. To get the most out of books and to ensure that reading together is a pleasurable experience for both parent and child, it is important to be able to vary your reading style and the choice of books on offer to fit with your child's level of attention, his abilities and interests. You may introduce different kinds of books to help stimulate your child's interest, for example, books of different size and texture, books with flaps, noises, big and small pictures. A trip to the library may help you investigate the variety of books available for young children. All the principles of child-centred communication apply when looking at books together:

- Establish a routine that allows for *your child's* choice of book as well as *your* choice of book.
- Snuggle up close together and position yourself so that your child can still see your face and the book easily.
- Encourage your child to hold the book with you and turn the pages gently.
- Watch and wait to see what your child is interested in on each page and go along with their interest, repeating and expanding their ideas.
- You do not have to stick with the text of the book. You can instead describe what's happening in the pictures at a level your child will understand. Point to the relevant pictures as you speak. This is especially important for children with learning difficulties in helping them understand and to pay attention.
- Using lots of interesting tones in your voice, emphasising new words and phrases and keeping your language clear and understandable will help your child pay attention to the book.
- Ask questions that will focus your child and stretch his imagination, for example, 'I wonder what will happen next?' or 'What would *you* do if you got a kite like the boy in the book?' *Wait* for a response. If the answer is brief or vague, you can repeat his idea in a longer clearer sentence. 'Sky' could be followed with 'Yes, you'd fly the kite up in the sky'.
- Conversations that arise naturally from a story in a book should be encouraged. Asking genuine questions and relating the information on the page to your child's own experiences is a powerful way of starting positive conversations and also helps your child's imaginative development.

2 Using Music and Songs

Parent and child can enjoy great moments of connection together through music and song. Making music part of your child's day can have multiple benefits:

I'M NOT SURE I BUY THIS 'YOU'RE WATCHING HIM WATCH TV SO YOU CAN SEE IF HE NEEDS HELP' LINE ... YOU LIKE THE TELLYTUBBIES YOURSELF, DON'T YOU?

- In learning songs the child is encouraged to look, listen, imitate, follow directions and anticipate.
- The tune of songs can help your child maintain interest and learn and remember new words.
- Action songs such as 'The Wheels on the Bus' or 'Head and Shoulders, Knees and Toes' are especially interesting to preschool children. As well as helping to release energy and express feelings in a positive way, action songs can also help their sense of rhythm, physical co-ordination and sequencing skills.
- Fingerplay songs such as 'This Little Piggie' and songs such as 'Ring Around the Rosie' can provide much fun. They are also very interactive as you both join in and young children learn to listen carefully to anticipate the ending of the song – tickling and jumping down.

47

Young children love to sing the same songs over and over again. The repetitive nature of children's songs helps them learn and remember the words and tune. Children will usually imitate body movements before words. To help your child learn the actions, stay close by, get down to her level and be face to face so that she can see your face clearly as you sing. You can guide her actions, using your hands to encourage her. Nursery rhyme picture books, drawing pictures about the songs, or involving toy figures to join in the music will all help your child make sense of the words she hears and make music interesting.

Ensure that singing familiar songs together with your child is interactive by going slowly and waiting to give your child an opportunity to practise. Leave pauses in the song for your child to fill if they can. Encourage your child's attempts as this will make it more likely that he will persist and continue.

Children and their parents can sing together anywhere at anytime. Singing together during 'tidy up', 'dressing in the morning' and other everyday routines encourages the child to relax and to keep with the task at hand. A great way of making difficult tasks enjoyable for young children is to make up a song to describe your actions as you go. To the tune of 'Twinkle, Twinkle' you could make up words relevant to your child's actions – arms up, arms through the sleeve, now jumper is on.

3 Creative Play Activities

Being creative in your time together is important as children are best motivated to learn when they are enjoying themselves. Activities such as painting, drawing, puppet play, playdough, cooking or gardening together can be highly enjoyable activities for both parents and children. While some parents make the most of everyday chores by turning them into games, for example, turning sorting the laundry into a matching game, others will set aside a particular time to support their child's creativity. The more new experiences you can introduce and get your child involved in, the more opportunities there are to learn and have fun together. By joining in and supporting your child in creative play activities you help them grow in confidence and to improve skills such as learning concepts, awareness of colours and shapes and social skills such as taking turns, sharing, and encouraging.

Ideas for playing together creatively

Making things together:
Make animals and other familiar things out of playdough.
Make handprints and potato prints on paper with paint.
Make paper planes, boats and trains.
Make hats from newspaper and decorate them.
Make puppets from old socks and draw a face on them.

Pretending together:
Build a tent out of blankets and towels.
Have a teddy bear picnic on the floor.
Play dressing-up and make-up.
Role-play, pretending to be at the shop/zoo/hospital.

Play together outside:
Go on a nature walk and collect leaves and flowers as you go.
Set up an 'obstacle' course.
Hide and seek with teddy in the garden.
Use chalk to draw on the path and play hopscotch.

Fun in everyday activities together:
Make rice crispie buns.
Plant seeds and water the plants.
Record your child singing or talking and listen back to it together.
Have a 'boat' race in a tub of water.

TIPS FOR GOING FORWARD

1   Pick an activity that your child is really interested in and use this to set up a learning opportunity for him or her.
2   Remember the stages of helping children learn:
    -   WAIT to let your child communicate first/ or come up with an idea.
    -   ACKNOWLEDGE your child's idea or REPEAT what your child says ('It's a Teddy').
    -   Give them a NEW IDEA or WORD. ('Teddy's sleeping').
    -   WAIT to see how your child responds.

STEP 4

THE IMPORTANCE OF ENCOURAGEMENT AND PRAISE

I realised recently that I could be very critical of my children, correcting them every time they did something wrong. Ironically, I was only doing it because I wanted the best for them. I wanted to make sure my children grew up behaving well and knowing right from wrong. But now I know that while my intentions were good I was on the wrong track. My children need my encouragement and praise much more than my criticism and correction. When I became more encouraging, I realised that it is not only the best way to teach them how to behave well, it also makes things much more positive in the family. I felt a lot closer and more positive about my children when I encouraged them.

People often think that the best way to change a child's misbehaviour is to criticise and scold them and to point out to them when they do something wrong. However, being critical causes a lot of problems – it can damage a child's confidence, it can make things negative between you and it gives attention to the misbehaviour. It is far more effective to become an encouraging parent – that is to go out of your way to notice and praise any examples of good behaviour you see and help your children learn what they are doing right and well. In addition, an encouraging parent is sensitive to their child's feelings and is always on the lookout for opportunities to affirm and value them.

Critical Parent	Encouraging Parent
'Don't put that there'	'Put it here/let me show you'
'That's not right'	'Try it like this'
'You're doing it wrong'	'Oh, you are trying hard aren't you'
'Don't get angry like that'	'I know you are upset at having to leave'
'Why didn't you pick the blue block?'	'Oh you picked the green block, you like green!'

THE BEST WAY TO ENCOURAGE

When we use encouragement or praise with children, we can make sure it gets through to the child by ensuring that it is clear, specific and personal.

Encouragement should be clear

You should have your child's full attention before you give encouraging statements. It is less effective to encourage with statements muttered under your breath from another part of the room or when your child is doing something else like watching a video and not really listening. It is important to get down to his level and make eye contact, using a warm and genuine tone of voice and backing up the words with a hug or pat on the back. Though words are important, your tone of voice and facial expression are crucial in ensuring your encouragement gets through. This is especially the case with young children with little language. Your child should be in no doubt that he or she is getting a positive message from you. Think of encouragement as the most important message you can possibly give to your children. You really want to make sure it gets through to them.

Encouragement should be specific

If you want to help children to change positively they need to know exactly which behaviour they are being praised for, and which qualities you are encouraging in them. Vague statements, such as, 'You are a great boy' or 'Good girl' don't tell a child what you are pleased about, and can soon wear thin and seem insincere. It is more effective to say, 'You put your socks on, good boy' or 'You gave Jean a crayon; good girl for sharing'. These statements help children know exactly what good behaviour you are praising and make it more likely to occur again. It is also important to praise as soon after the desired behaviour as possible so they are in no doubt that it is that behaviour you want to see again.

Encouragement should be personal

The best way to encourage is unique to each parent and child. What is essential though, is that your child experiences your encouragement as personal and genuine. Rather than it being a technique, encouragement is about a moment of connection between parent and child. Different approaches work for different children. Some like a big deal made, for others a simple hug or a pat on the back can speak volumes. Remember, what works in encouragement varies from parent to parent and from child to child. Find out what works for you.

Encourage small steps

Often parents say that they never witness examples of the good behaviour they want in their children because the children never do what they're asked, or they never share with other children. When you are feeling negative and angry it can be hard to notice the positives. However, if you closely observe your children you will notice that there are always times, however short-lived, when they are behaving more positively. If you are serious about helping your children change, it can make a real difference to notice these exceptions. Children need to know there are some things they are doing right, before they can have the confidence to change.

It is important not to wait for perfection or a finished task before you encourage or praise. Change can be gradual and, to ensure that children don't get demotivated, it is important to encourage and praise steps in the right direction. For example, encourage a child when she *starts* to put her toys away in the box or when she *starts* to put on her socks to get dressed. You don't have to wait for the task to be completed. Encouraging the first step of a task helps a child persist and continue to the end.

Double Encouragement

Involving other people can double the effect of encouragement. Praising a child in public or in front of important people can make it more powerful and really drive the message home. For example, if Dad has witnessed good behaviour, as well as praising it himself he can double the impact by telling Mum about it in front of the child later in the day. There is often a tendency to nag about misbehaviour, to really go on about what is wrong. Using encouragement, you can turn this around and really emphasise what your child has done right. Tell both the child and those involved in the family how pleased you are with what the child has done. You can even use the phone as the mother did below:

> My son loves other people to know when he has done something right. I remember when he first went to the toilet by himself (which was a big achievement), we made sure to ring not only his Daddy at work, but also

his Aunty Jackie! He was so excited as he tried to tell them on the phone what happened and it really made a difference as he continued to use the toilet without a problem. We always use the phone now when he does something really good. It is great because it is really immediate and he really feels proud of himself.

Persist with Encouragement

Adopting an encouraging stance towards your children can sometimes be very difficult. If you have been dealing with misbehaviour and problems from your child for a long time, you may feel angry and upset and maintain feelings of negativity towards her. In these situations, it can be hard to notice the good qualities in your child and you can easily miss her good behaviour as it seems to occur so infrequently.

In addition, some children respond less well to encouragement than others. This is especially the case for children with social skills difficulties or who have autistic traits, which makes it difficult for them to absorb praise. In these situations it is worth persisting and finding ways of getting your encouragement through, as the father in the next example discovered.

My son has an autistic spectrum disorder and as a result he can be quite distant and caught up in his own world. When I tried to encourage or interact with him, he seemed not to care and I could easily feel hurt. Through attending a parenting course I learnt that I had to do things differently to get through to him. I needed first to join with him in whatever he was playing (he was obsessed by dinosaurs) and then once I had his attention I could build on this. I also learnt that I had to be much more upbeat and positive when encouraging him to do something. I had to make eye contact, use a very upbeat tone of voice and put a lot of energy in to get his attention. Though it took a bit of effort, my son began to respond and I was able to make a connection with him. It's not perfect but we are making progress.

UNDERSTANDING FEELINGS

A crucial part of making encouragement work is being able to appreciate your child's feelings, while communicating your own feelings in turn. In the long term, the aim is to help children understand their own and other people's feelings. Talking about and teaching young children about feelings has a number of benefits for parents and children alike:

1　Being sensitive to and appreciating your children's feelings is a great way to connect with them and to 'tune into their world'.

2　Acknowledging children's feelings when they protest or don't want to do something can help them feel understood and thus help them cooperate.

3　Teaching children about their own feelings and those of others helps them learn how to make friends and get on with other children and adults.

4   Helping children understand and communicate their own angry and upset feelings reduces misbehaviour such as tantrums or aggression.

Communicating such understanding and appreciation of children's feelings is a powerful way of promoting their emotional security and teaching them empathy.

YOU'RE HAPPY BECAUSE I'M TAKING THE TIME TO HELP YOU EXPRESS FEELINGS LIKE 'HAPPY'...

The best way to teach the language of feelings

Like words, feelings are hard for young children to recognise and understand and they need a lot of help from their parents. The best way to teach the language of feelings is to *notice, name* and *comment* when your child experiences a strong feeling. This works best if you:

- Get down to your child's level and make eye contact.
- Reflect the feeling back, 'You like being tickled' or 'Oh, you are sad'.
- Imitate your child's facial expression. If he is smiling you smile, if he frowns you frown.
- Mirror his body language. If he claps when excited you clap!
- Name the feeling verbally, emphasising the key word, 'Oh, you're sad because we have to leave.'
- Use a sad tone of voice for a sad feeling and a happy tone of voice for a happy one.

Remember, feelings are mainly communicated through tone of voice and facial expression and less through words.

Examples

- If you see your child smiling when playing, a good idea is to get down to his level, match the smile on his face and say:

    'Oh, you're *smiling*, you like playing with *Teddy*.'

- If your child is getting frustrated with making a tower you can get down to his level and sympathetically say:

    'Oh, its *hard* to do this jigsaw. Will Daddy help you?'

- If your child is shy meeting a stranger, you can get down to his level and whisper:

    'I know it's hard to talk to people you don't know.'

Then take the pressure off your child by giving him some more information:

    'This is my friend Barbara.'

Acknowledging a child's protests

Acknowledging your child's feelings (without giving in) when he protests about a rule is a good way to help him cooperate:

    'Oh, I know you want to watch the video (using a sad voice), but it is time to go to Nana's house now (upbeat voice).'

If your child scrunches up her face as you try to wash it, you can say:

> 'You don't like that (you scrunch your face too),
> but we have to clean your face because (upbeat)
> then we can go out.'

If your child refuses to give you a hug, rather than being critical, or 'hurt' you can be 'light' and acknowledge your child's feelings:

> 'Oh, I guess you don't feel like a hug right now.'

Share your own feelings

You can teach your child about feelings by making sure to tell them about yours:

- 'Mummy feels tired now and needs to sleep.'
- 'Daddy is cross because the toys are not tidied away yet.'

Talk about other children's feelings

It can also help to talk about what other children are feeling during an incident.

- 'Brian (baby brother) is upset because he wants to play too.'

Talk about feelings when reading books and stories

Books provide a good way of teaching feelings and helping children learn how to make friends and deal with problems.

- 'Little bear felt sad because someone took his toy.'
- 'Grandma was very happy because Sam ate all his dinner up.'

Managing misbehaviour and distressing feelings

Much of young children's misbehaviour is caused when they experience overwhelming feelings of anger and upset that they don't understand. It can help if you can name and contain these feelings and then find ways to soothe your children in their distress. This can be as simple as saying, 'You're feeling angry because you can't go out' or 'You're feeling tired and you need a nap' and then to comfort the child in a calm way. We will discuss later in Part 2 of the book how you can manage your child's feelings (as well as your own) during difficult discipline situations:

> My three-year-old daughter could get cranky and annoyed just before bedtime. I saw her as 'just being difficult' and would often react angrily which could lead to a row. Things changed when I tried to be a bit more sensitive to her feelings (as well as my own). Instead of reacting, I would try and respond sensitively, acknowledging that she was tired or upset going to bed. Taking time to listen to her feelings did make a difference.

TIPS FOR GOING FORWARD

1 Make a list of all the good things your children do and the positive qualities you like to see in them.
2 Go out of your way to notice anytime your children behave well or anytime they do something you like.
3 Make a point of noticing and commenting on your children's feelings.
4 Be encouraging towards yourself as a parent – rather than giving yourself a hard time, make a point of noticing occasions when you do something well.

STEP 5

TEACHING CHILDREN NEW TASKS AND ROUTINES

It used to take ages getting my daughter dressed in the morning and it could end up in a row because I would be under pressure to get going. When I thought about it, I realised that I was doing everything for my daughter – when she was probably capable of doing most of the dressing tasks herself. I decided then to give her more of the responsibility for dressing and to be there to support and teach her. Of course this took longer at first, but in the end she began to dress herself. Not only was she proud of this, but it took all the pressure off me in the morning.

In earlier parts of the book we talked of how important it is for parents to tune into their children and to follow their children's lead, especially in child-centred play. This is only half the story as it is also important for parents to be able to take the lead with their children. As a parent you have to get your children to cooperate with basic tasks throughout the day such as dressing, eating breakfast, going to preschool, eating dinner and going to bed, to name but a few! However, you can still use the important skill of tuning in to your child as you take the lead throughout the day. The more you understand your child's feelings, thoughts and interests the more you will be able to gently guide and encourage him. Below are some ideas on how to 'take the lead' with children during tasks and routines.

PLAN IN ADVANCE

Think in advance of what situations you need to take a lead with your child in and plan how you are going to approach them. Sometimes simple routine changes can make a big difference. For example, one mother described how her daughter would become uncooperative getting dressed in the morning if she tried to dress her downstairs when the TV was on. As a result the mother changed the routine and insisted her child got dressed upstairs before she came down to the TV. Another father found it better to have a quiet reading time with his son before bedtime, instead of physical play, which used to make his son hyperactive and uncooperative about bedtime.

Plan to have enough time

Make sure you have enough time especially with a difficult task. Rushing only makes things difficult. For example, if the morning routine is a problem, get up a little earlier when you will have more time to guide your child in how to get dressed and make it a fun activity. When your child gets more comfortable with the routine you will be able to do it more quickly.

Involve the children in the task

Try to involve children in the activity you want them to do and give them choices, 'Oh we have to tidy up now. Mummy will help. Do you want to put away the blocks or the animals?'

Try and make the task fun!

Try and make the exercise fun and creative; when tidying up you can sing the Barney 'Clean Up' song, for instance, or have a race to see who can put the toys away first. This means going a little bit slower to take time to teach your child new things or to enjoy the experience. The more you can make the task an enjoyable shared experience between you and your child the easier it will be.

Notice when your child cooperates

Comment on and describe any times your child helps or cooperates. Consider the following 'Oh, we're putting your coat on to go out... that's right you put your hand in the sleeve. That's a big help' or 'You're waiting so quietly for me at the doctor's. That makes me very happy.'

Acknowledge feelings

If your child is a little unhappy about the task, it can be helpful to acknowledge her feelings. But it is important to do this in an upbeat way, and not scold a child for being uncooperative. For example, if your child protests as he comes in from playing in the garden you can say (using an emphatic tone of voice) 'I know you want to play in the garden, but it is time to come in for dinner now ... we're having ice-cream for dessert!' (finishing with an upbeat tone of voice).

Be calm and upbeat

If your child does continue to protest and whine, it is important that you don't respond angrily by lecturing or giving out as this can fuel your child's protests. Rather it is important not to let these get to you and to focus calmly on getting the task done. Be aware of your own tone of voice, keeping it friendly and calm. Even if your child gets angry or upset do not rise to this and get upset yourself. *Remember to be an assertive parent by being calm, friendly and firm.*

Be encouraging

Use lots of praise and encouragement as the child carries out the task, 'Thank you for getting in the car when Mummy asked.

You are a good boy' or 'You let Alice play as well; you're very kind' and back this up with smiles, hugs and warm touches (especially important for children with little language).

Follow a difficult task with an enjoyable activity

Try to follow an activity which requires your child's cooperation with another activity which is more rewarding for the child, 'Oh, now that we've tidied everything away, I've time to read you a story' or 'Oh, now that you've finished your dinner, we can go out and play'. This is especially important with tasks that your child doesn't like. Focusing on the reward afterwards can be enough to get the job done.

HELPING CHILDREN LEARN TO DO DAILY TASKS BY THEMSELVES

In the long term, the aim is to help children learn how to do the daily tasks by themselves. Even young children can begin to learn basic self-care tasks at an early age such as dressing, putting on shoes, washing teeth. They may not be able to do the whole task but they can do part of it such as putting a sock on, or fastening straps. It is a good idea to encourage children to begin to do these tasks *as early as possible and as soon as they are ready to learn*. This not only helps children learn independence and become confident, but it can also reduce conflict and rows. They are less likely to resist when they are involved and more likely to feel proud when they complete the task.

However, it is important to remember that children don't automatically know how to do these tasks and have to learn them slowly over time. You can think of your job as a parent like that of teacher, taking time to teach your children these basic tasks and skills when they are ready to learn them.

Helping a child learn a new task

1 Wait and watch your child. Is he ready to learn this new skill?
2 Show your child how to do the task, describing in simple language what you are doing.
3 Give your child a turn and watch to see if they can do it, while you comment in an encouraging way on what they are doing.
4 If your child needs some help, give some gentle physical assistance (hand over hand), and comment on what you are both doing.
5 Now back off and let your child practise his new skill, while you continue to encourage and praise him.

Teaching children using hand over hand

Learning new things such as how to complete a jigsaw or how to dress or feed yourself can be a difficult and often frustrating task for children. To allow children to learn new activities in a successful way they may need some gentle physical assistance from their parents. This can be done by first watching your child's efforts and seeing if they need your help, and then placing your hand over your child's hand, guiding them through the movements if necessary. You might also comment on what you are both doing, – 'We're turning the handle so the door will open' or 'We're being very gentle so the piece won't fall.'

It is important that you take time to watch your child first to see if he requires your help and so avoid overuse of physical prompts and to encourage his independence. By making successful attempts at new activities a child gains confidence as well as new skills. The more experience children have at being successful, the more likely they are to persist at more difficult tasks. In turn, increased time spent exploring an activity helps children to develop their concentration skills. By taking your child's hand and teaching him new skills you offer a special opportunity for your child to connect with you.

ESTABLISHING ROUTINES

Sequencing daily events in the same way at a set time helps young children in many ways. It can also make life a little easier for their parents!

Establishing a good, consistent daily routine for your child at mealtimes, bedtime and bathtime helps your child to anticipate and predict what is next, and also helps her learn when things start and finish. When your child is sure of what is expected, it is more likely that she will co-operate. Rewards, such as a story after pyjamas are put on or a trip to the park after a long wait in the shops, can be a natural part of the routine .

Good routines also allow children to develop other skills such as planning ahead, anticipating and self-discipline. When children learn the next step in the sequence this helps them to make choices for themselves, thus promoting independence.

Examples of a bedtime routine:
- Washing hands, face and teeth.
- Putting pyjamas on.
- Listening to a story.
- Turning off the lights.

As you help your child establish a routine you can comment on what they have done so far and what there is still to do, 'Good boy, you've washed yourself. Now you need to put your pyjamas on' or 'We'll read a story, then it's time to sleep'.

Other simple routines:
- Tidy away one toy before playing with the next.
- Turn off the TV before mealtime.

Using pictures to teach new skills and explain routines

Children who have difficulty in understanding the spoken word will quickly learn routines from observing and taking part in the routine. Planning a schedule together through pictures also serves as a good point of reference for your child to focus on, especially if they are easily distracted, confused or have difficulty in understanding language. Creating pictures together to explain routines and teach new skills also allows you and your child to share and create something together, and helps you plan ahead with your child instead of teaching them under pressure.

Breaking routines into manageable steps that are visible through pictures can help explain daily routines at mealtimes, bedtimes and also more problematic events such as going shopping in town, visiting the hospital and babysitting.

Pictures can be used in numerous ways to help teach your child new skills and routines. For example, teaching your child a new kind of game, or how to take turns during play or to use the toilet.

WITH A LITTLE PRACTICE, MAKING PICTURES TO HELP OUR CHILD LEARN ROUTINES HAS BECOME ROUTINE!

Creating Picture Routines

- Draw and cut out a series of pictures together with your child to explain a routine or skill that you would like your child to understand and learn. Don't worry about being an expert artist. The pictures are merely a back up for your explanation to your child.

- If your child is able and interested, you can involve him in the drawing of the pictures, or you can draw them as you sit with him and explain the routine. The more you involve your child the more interested he will be.
- Write a clear sentence under each picture to explain what should happen.
- Make sure not to have too many pictures on one page. For a young child, have only one picture per page and bind them together like a little book.
- Get your child's attention to explain the sequence of pictures, pointing to each picture in turn. The pictures can be explained as if reading a story to your child.
- Keep the picture schedule close by so that it can be referred to easily.
- As each part of the sequence is complete, make it clear that it is finished and focus your child on the next step. Explain, for example, 'We're finished dinner now, so it's time to collect your brother from school', pointing to the relevant pictures. (For younger children and those who have difficulty in understanding language you could simply say, 'Dinner finished; Let's get Johnny.')
- It is useful to have something rewarding at the end of the sequence, such as playtime or book time, to keep your child motivated.

My three-year-old is very energetic and gets bored easily so when we were due to go on a long flight I was dreading it. We got the idea to prepare him for the trip using a picture book. I divided up all the stages of the journey (going to the airport, checking in the bags, getting on the plane, watching a movie, arriving) and drew a picture with my son for each stage. My son was really interested in the pictures and I made sure that there was something for him to do at each stage (packing his bag, carrying his ticket, doing puzzles on the plane). This preparation made all the difference, and got him involved. When we took the flight he took the picture book with him and we followed each of the stages.

Picture Routines Examples

We have four sample routines drawn out for you. (See page 71, 72)

1 Taking turns in a game.
2 Getting dressed.
3 A daily routine of collecting a brother from school.
4 An explanation of mother being away on a trip.

TIPS FOR GOING FORWARD

1 Identify a task or chore that your child might be ready to learn.
2 Do up a picture schedule of the stages involved and show these to your child.
3 Use lots of encouragement and praise as your child learns the task.

Picture Routines Examples

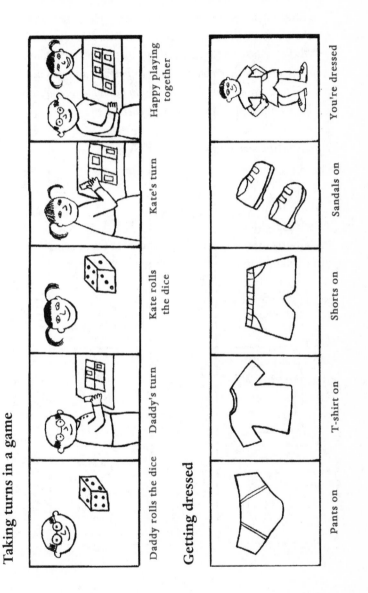

Taking turns in a game

Daddy rolls the dice | Daddy's turn | Kate rolls the dice | Kate's turn | Happy playing together

Getting dressed

Pants on | T-shirt on | Shorts on | Sandals on | You're dressed

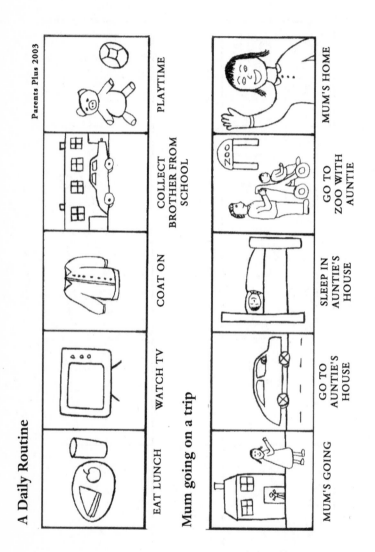

A Daily Routine

Parents Plus 2003

EAT LUNCH · WATCH TV · COAT ON · COLLECT BROTHER FROM SCHOOL · PLAYTIME

Mum going on a trip

MUM'S GOING · GO TO AUNTIE'S HOUSE · SLEEP IN AUNTIE'S HOUSE · GO TO ZOO WITH AUNTIE · MUM'S HOME

Part 2
Teaching Children to Behave Well

STEP 6

RESPONDING TO MISBEHAVIOUR

Jack (6) and his sister Julie (4) used to fight and squabble all the time. Their parents found themselves being drawn in as referees to the fights and often everyone involved would get upset. They felt they couldn't leave the children alone for a moment without a fight breaking out.

In the first part of this book we emphasised the importance of positive parenting (involving positive attention, play, encouragement and praise) as great ways to develop a good relationship with children, and to help them learn and develop and to reach their full potential.

But this is not the full story. Young children often misbehave in different ways such as with tantrums, defiance, aggression, running off and so on, and these are difficult things to manage for parents, often causing rows and conflict. And while there is no magic solution that works every time (unfortunately!), there are a number of principles to bear in mind that can make a real difference in minimising the upset for you and your child. Following these pointers will help you to get through a difficult situation safely and respectfully while helping your child learn how to behave well in the long term.

UNDERSTANDING MISBEHAVIOUR
Children misbehave for a whole variety of reasons, such as looking for attention, expressing frustration or hurt, or wanting to take control. Sometimes it can occur as a battle of wills or a

power struggle when your child comes head to head with you because he wants to get his own way. Sometimes misbehaviour occurs in an ongoing context such as a child feeling jealous of a younger brother or because a child is struggling in pre-school. Children with special needs often misbehave because they know of no other way to communicate. For example, a child with little language may hit out because he does not have the words to ask for what he wants; or a child with attention problems will find it hard to remember to keep rules; or a child with autistic traits may throw a tantrum when his routine is changed because he finds change very hard to manage.

TEACHING CHILDREN HOW TO BEHAVE

A good way to think about misbehaviour and many childhood problems is to see that a child has not yet learnt the skill of how to behave well. For example, a child grabs a toy because he has not learnt how to share yet. Or a child with special needs hits out when frustrated because she has not yet learnt how to communicate how she feels. You can see it as your job as a parent to teach your children the skills of behaving well. For example, if your two children are always fighting, think of ways you can help them learn how to share and get along with one another. Or if your child finds it hard to concentrate on tasks, think of things you can do to help him learn how to concentrate.

RESPONDING TO MISBEHAVIOUR

In the first part of the book we emphasised how important it is to be a responsive rather than a reactive parent – the key is to be sensitive and 'in tune' with your child as well as aware of your own feelings so that you can choose the best response in any situation. This principle applies especially to handling misbehaviour. Whatever the problem you are facing it is a good idea to be proactive and responsive. Rather than letting it happen over and over again, it is a good idea to take time to think through how you want to respond and to come up with a plan of action. As we described in Step 1 you can try the following:

1 Pausing.
2 'Tune into' your child.
3 'Tune into' yourself.
4 Choosing your response.

Pause and think before you act

In the first part of the book we talked of the importance of taking time to tune into your children and to understand where they are coming from in play and learning situations. This pausing and thinking is equally important in discipline situations – though it can be difficult when emotions are high. It is a good idea not to immediately react when your child does something wrong, but to pause and think through the best way to respond. The question becomes, 'What is the best way to deal with this situation so that my child will learn how to behave well in the future?'

With an ongoing problem, it is useful to set aside some time to think through (either by yourself or in discussion with a partner or friend) what is going on and to come up with a plan of action.

Tune into your child

Before you respond it is a good idea to think first about what might be going on for your child. You want to tune into what your child might be thinking and feeling and this will allow you to choose the best response. When faced by your son's tantrum, for example, it is a good idea to wonder whether this is due to him feeling tired or upset or is he having the tantrum to get his own way and avoid going to bed. You can't really know how best to respond until you've paused for a moment and asked yourself, 'What is really going on here? What is the best way to respond?' This is what we mean by tuning in first.

Tune into yourself

Before you respond it is equally important to become aware of your own feelings and needs and to reflect about what is going on for you. For example, is the misbehaviour caused by your own unrealistic expectations? Maybe the behaviour is pretty normal for a child of this age, or maybe it is understandable in the context of his special needs or stage of development. Some honest self-reflection is called for.

What matters most in discipline situations is how you manage your own emotions. If you become angry or upset, you will find it hard to think clearly, and are likely to react angrily to your child which is generally not helpful. All discipline responses are best carried out in a calm, assertive manner. This does not happen easily. Being calm in difficult situations where you feel upset, hurt or angry is possibly the hardest thing of all to do. If your child snaps angrily at you, it is hard not to match this anger and to snap back, especially if you feel he is being abusive. Or if you are out in the supermarket when your child throws a tantrum, you can feel humiliated and upset because of the audience present, and this can cause you to react angrily.

Choosing your response

At this point the goal is to think up as many possible responses as possible that will allow you to manage the misbehaviour effectively and safely and which will help your children learn to behave well in the long term. Choosing the best response depends on the situation in question. Take, for example, a situation in which your son has a tantrum late at night:

- This could simply be due to him being tired, suggesting the correct response is a gentle distraction to go to bed.
- Or it could result from him being upset; a suitable response is one which soothes him and acknowledges his feelings.
- Or he could be using the tantrum as a means to get his own way, suggesting it might be best to ignore him until he calms down.

When coming up with solutions, the important thing is to be as creative as possible and to think up as many answers as possible. Often you may have to try different strategies in succession. If your child is hitting out when playing with other children, you can take time to teach him how to play with others, as well as implementing a clear consequence (such as 'Time Out') if he hits out again.

BE FLEXIBLE

It is important to remember that no strategy or response works all the time and as children grow up you may have to change how you respond and be flexible. Dealing with misbehaviour and problems can be hard work and you have to be prepared to use lots of different strategies depending on your child and what works best with him in a given situation. Different things work with different children and this is especially the case with children with special needs.

For example, sometimes it can be useful to ignore a child's protests and calmly insist. At other times it can be useful to pause and acknowledge their feelings, or again you might need to give a child an upbeat distraction to do something else. What matters is that you take time to pause and think before reacting.

You need to tune into your child and think what will work here and now with him?

POSSIBLE RESPONSES TO MISBEHAVIOUR

Below we list possible responses to misbehaviour that have been researched as useful in many parenting situations. Each of these responses will be explored in more detail in the remaining chapters of the book. Remember no single response works every time or with every child. What matters is that you think through what will work best with your child, and be prepared to change your responses if they are not working.

Responses to Misbehaviour

Step 7   Praising good behaviour and ignoring misbehaviour.
              Listening to your Child/ Naming and Managing Feelings.

Step 8   Assertively tell your child what you want.
              Distract your child with a new activity.

Step 9   Use Choices and Consequences.
              Time Out – A special consequence.

Step 10   Teaching children how to behave using rewards and books.

RESPONDING TO MISBEHAVIOUR

Now to illustrate some of these ideas lets revisit the problem of children squabbling and fighting introduced at the beginning of the chapter.

Squabbles and fights

> Jack (6) and his sister Julie (4) used to fight and squabble all the time. Their parents found themselves being drawn in as referees to the fights and often all involved would become upset. They felt they couldn't leave the children alone for a moment without a fight breaking out.

When the parents took time to think about what was going on they realised that many of the fights were due to the two children being close in age and jealous of each other. They also realised that their own response of acting as referees was not helping them sort it out themselves. As a result they decided to respond in a number of different ways.

1 To address the jealousy, they made sure to give each child individual time with each parent as well as time together – Step 1.
2 They took time to help the children play with one another (by sitting with them and guiding them as they played) – Step 1 and 2.
3 They also went out of their way to notice and encourage the children any time they 'caught' them sharing or playing alongside one another – Step 3.
4 They did up a reward chart with the two children, giving them a star anytime they played well together – Step 10.
5 When the children got into a fight, rather than getting into an argument about who was at fault, they would ignore this and remind the children to behave well – Step 7.

6   If they continued to fight, they would give them a warning before insisting they went to their rooms for a 'Time Out' – Step 9.

TIPS FOR GOING FORWARD

1   Think of a time when your child misbehaves or of a problem in your family that you would like to solve.

2   Take a moment to 'tune into' the situation – What is going on for your children and yourself that gives rise to the problem? What does your child need to learn? How do you want to respond differently?

3   Choose a new way of responding to the situation that might work better.

STEP 7

THE POWER OF ATTENTION

Bed-time with four-year-old Zoe was a nightmare. She just would not settle by herself and would insist on story after story from her parents. First, she wanted her Dad to read and then her Mum. When they would leave her she would cry until they came back or she would come down the stairs saying she was thirsty or the room was too cold or too hot. Her parents would go up to sort this out and then she would want something else. It was endless. Her parents would resort to lecturing, cajoling and bribing her to stay in her room, with just 'one more story' or 'another five minutes downstairs'. Both Zoe and her parents would become exhausted and sometimes very upset.

Have you noticed how young children will do anything to get their parents' attention? Having their parents notice and respond to them is probably the greatest reward for children and they will seek this in as many ways as possible. Often parents find ways of giving approving, loving attention to their children, with warm hugs, close conversations and kind words. These are good habits and are very healthy for parent and child. Unfortunately, parents often unwittingly provide attention negatively via shouting, criticising and even slapping. Strange as it may seem, for many children these negative interactions are preferable to no attention at all and children will seek them out if they are being ignored for positive behaviour.

In the example above, Zoe is getting lots of attention from her parents for not going to bed. If she makes a fuss she gets extra stories, extra time awake with her parents and can even persuade her parents to sit in the bed with her. You'd wonder why she would want to change this at all! In this situation her parents can make some simple changes in how they respond to Zoe at night-time that could make a real difference. For example, they could:

1 Set up a routine at night (which they keep!) that specifies at what time she goes to bed, how many stories she get, and at what time they leave her in her room.

2 Ensure she gets lots of praise when she goes to bed on time, or gets into the bed as asked and gets lots of positive attention during storytime.

3 Ensure she gets little attention when she gets out of bed or asks for something. The parents could firmly guide her back to her bed without saying much at all.

4 Ensure she gets no extra rewards such as an extra story or extra time up when she gets out of the bed, but is simply brought back to her room.

5 The parents could also use a star chart to encourage her and to give her extra praise and attention to stay in her bed (see Step 10).

Using attention giving to your advantage

A powerful way to teach children how to behave well is to go out of your way to pay attention to them any time you see them behaving positively or doing what you want, while at the same time withdrawing your attention and ignoring most of their misbehaviour. For example, if you are concerned about your children squabbling and rowing and you find yourself getting drawn in as a referee (and thus inadvertently giving attention to bad behaviour), you could decide to switch this around and do things differently – instead you could largely ignore the squabbling and go out of your way to notice and attend to your children anytime they get on with each other. Any time you see them sharing a game or playing quietly you could go over and join them and say, 'It's nice to see you sharing a game' or 'It's good to see you both getting on'.

The trick is to switch your attention from noticing what is wrong and to notice what is going right. Instead of trying to catch your children out for being naughty you are trying to catch them being good. In Step 4 we described the best ways to go about encouraging children so that it gets through to them and helps them learn how to behave well.

Ignoring misbehaviour

As well as attending to positive behaviour, the second part of the equation is to withdraw your attention from misbehaviour and to pay it as little attention as possible. Ignoring misbehaviour is about not lecturing and scolding children or not getting drawn into rows (all forms of attention which could prolong the row), but instead remaining calm and attending to something else.

Ignoring could mean calmly sitting out a young child's tantrum, not responding to a child's nagging, calmly getting on with a job despite a child's whining or not paying attention to a sulking child. To be able to ignore you shouldn't take misbehaviour personally and dwell on it. While a child's misbehaviour can be very upsetting, good ignoring is about not letting it get to you, or not holding on to it, but moving on from it quickly to find examples of good behaviour you want.

Ignoring is definitely not easy. In fact it may be the hardest idea introduced in this book. Many parents think they are ignoring a behaviour but are inadvertently giving it attention via their body language, for example, by looking stern or disapproving, or by the fact that they are getting annoyed or emotional. While the child is receiving this type of unconscious attention the behaviour will continue. Equally, the silent treatment or not talking to your child for the day is not active ignoring. Indeed, such strategies can be counter-productive, building up resentment in both parent and child.

Examples of effective ignoring include:

- Parent ignores a child (by turning away) who is throwing a tantrum and only returns positive attention when child begins to come out of this.
- Parent holding a young whining child on lap, briefly turns away waiting for child to stop whining. When she does parent returns attention with a positive smile.
- When playing with two children, the younger one begins to get annoyed and grabs a toy. Rather than attend to this child, the parent first attends to the older child who has continued to play quietly and cooperatively. Robbed of any attention, the younger child gives back the toy. The parent immediately turns back positive attention, complimenting the child for his action.

It is possible to ignore misbehaviour while still interacting with the child. For example, if a child is whingeing because he doesn't want to put his coat on, the parent just says:

'We're putting your coat on. It's time to go.'

They then proceed to help the child put on her coat, before calmly guiding the child out the door. The parent does not get agitated, provoked or drawn into discussion or argument.

As well as ignoring young children when they misbehave, sometimes we also need to tell them what they can do instead. For example, if a child is screaming you might say:

'I'll talk to you when you speak quietly.'

This lets the child know what he needs to do to behave well. The crucial thing about ignoring is to stop yourself becoming angry or upset by the misbehaviour. This can be the hardest part. It can help to turn away and relax and to think of something positive in your mind or to practise deep breathing. Find something that works for you.

Return positive attention as soon as possible

When a child does give up the negative behaviour, such as when a tantrum stops, it is important to return positive attention, perhaps with a distraction or the suggestion of some positive activity. This is often not easy as the parent may be angry and upset after a period of misbehaviour and may use the opportunity now that the child is 'quiet' to scold or give out to her. However, this can restart the misbehaviour and stop the child learning the value of good positive behaviour.

Active ignoring only really works *when it is completed with a return of positive attention*. For example, if you notice your three-year-old daughter throws a tantrum because she wasn't allowed play with an inappropriate 'toy' like a sharp scissors. When you notice her coming out of the tantrum, rather than lecturing her about the original behaviour and thereby running the risk of reopening the argument, this is a good time to suggest a new activity in an upbeat positive manner. You could say for example, 'Oh, now you can play with the Lego or the crayons' or 'I think it might be time to make some lunch – would you like to help?' The point is that you are looking for a way to move on quickly from the original problem and to help your child get back on track with positive behaviour.

Listen to your Child

Ignoring is not a replacement for positive attention and encouragement (this is the most valuable aspect of parenting). Indeed there are many situations when it is inappropriate to ignore a child. For example, if your son is crying because he has been hurt or is worried about something, then maybe what he needs is to be soothed and comforted by you, or for you to listen carefully to what has happened, acknowledging his feelings. Many instances of misbehaviour are caused when a child experiences overwhelming feelings of anger and upset that they don't understand. Sometimes it is helpful to listen to a child for a period when they are misbehaving and to acknowledge their feelings. For example, a two-year-old child might throw a tantrum because she is simply very tired. In this instance a hug or a sympathetic face, perhaps saying, 'I know you're tired', might help her come round.

It is important to note that listening and acknowledging feelings is not about giving in or arguing. For example, you can sympathetically acknowledge that your son does not want to turn off the TV, but you are still insisting he does so. Or you can appreciate your daughter wanting to stay up later, but she still goes to bed on time. Listening, however, helps children feel understood and heard and thus helps them cooperate.

To listen or ignore?

Listening or soothing an upset child is a different approach to ignoring. Whether listening or ignoring works best depends on the situation you find yourself in and what you and your child are feeling. For example, when a child is intent on arguing with you to get his own way or when you find yourself angry then it may be more useful to ignore the child for a brief period until you and your child are more able to listen without arguing. Alternately, ignoring a child's cries can also be unhelpful if all the child needs at that time is to be heard or hugged and soothed. This is where pausing to tune into your child (and to yourself) can make a difference. By taking time to understand what is going on for your child first, you can decide which response is best.

The crucial test is to reflect on whether your attention is making the situation worse or better. Is the attention you are providing increasing or decreasing your child's distress? For example, if your child is sulking because he can't have a toy and you talk to him about it only to find him more angry, then maybe it is a good decision to give him more space. You can talk to him later when there is a better chance of a more constructive conversation, or to distract him with a new activity.

Ignoring is essentially about you being in charge of your own responses. It is about being able to choose not to respond negatively and being able to choose how and when you respond positively to your child.

A question of timing

Often, it is simply a question of timing. When children are very angry or frustrated, they are often not available to be soothed and need some time to calm down before a parent can soothe and support them. Sometimes ignoring and listening are intertwined. Consider the following:

- Parent gives an instruction ('You can't go out because it is dark').
- Child gets very angry and begins to sulk and whine.
- Parent ignores the sulking.
- Child begins to calm down and looks back to parent.
- Parent returns attention, naming the child's feelings, 'I know you're upset because you can't go out... its ok.'
- Child is more calm.
- Parent returns attention with a distraction, 'Look, let's play a game with your Lego'.

Listen to your own feelings

It is very useful to become aware of your own feelings in difficult discipline situations. If you notice when you are becoming stressed or angry, you can make a decision to pull back or to change how you are responding. Being aware of your feelings will help you make the best response. Sometimes sharing feelings with children can be helpful:

> 'Look, I'm getting annoyed now... I want you to come in.'
> 'I feel upset when you shout at me; please use a quiet voice.'

The power of attention

Shifting your attention from exclusively focusing on misbehaviour to focus on good behaviour and what is going well can make a real difference. Consider the situation described below:

> I was dealing with angry behaviour from my four-year-old son for many months. He could be particularly aggressive towards his younger brother. I was worn out by his behaviour and felt very negative towards him, and very bad about myself as a parent for feeling this way. When I went to the clinic they made a video of me playing with my two children and I noticed how I was unconsciously giving my younger son much more positive attention. Though my older son often did some things right, I missed these as I was expecting him to misbehave. I tended only to give him attention when he did something wrong. With the help of the clinic staff I was encouraged to turn this round. I went out of my way to be more positive towards my older son and to give him lots of positive attention when he behaved well, particularly when he was with his little brother. Though it was hard work to change, it began to make a difference. I came to appreciate how difficult things were for my older son on the birth of his brother and how he needed a lot of special attention to compensate.

TIPS FOR GOING FORWARD

1 Target one or two forms of behaviour which you can actively ignore during the coming week in order to eliminate them (for example, whinging and protesting).

2 Identify the positive opposite forms of behaviour and plan to encourage, praise and reward them each time they occur (when your child does what they are asked quietly and without protest).

3 Take time out to relax next week.

4 Visualise yourself calmly responding to a discipline problem, and not giving attention to the misbehaviour.

STEP 8

SETTING RULES WITH CHILDREN

Because my child would often misbehave, I found myself often correcting him, telling him 'not to do this' and 'not to do that'. A big insight for me was switching from using 'don'ts' to 'do's'. Now, rather than just correcting him I try to tell him what I want him to do instead. If he is annoying his sister I ask him to 'please play nicely' or 'to play with something else'. Though it is hard to remember to do it, such a simple change has made a big difference as he is more likely to do what I ask and it feels less confrontational.

THE BEST WAY TO SET RULES

Though in the first part of the book we emphasised the importance of being child-centred and following children's lead in play and activities, there are many situations where a parent has to set rules and to take the lead with their children. In this section, we look at some effective strategies to get children to cooperate and to keep rules that are child-centred and respectful.

Keep Rules to a Minimum

Generally, it is best to encourage children to make as many decisions for themselves as possible. As a result, it is important to keep the rules you set with children to a minimum, confining them to those that really matter. It is worth sitting down and thinking through what things are important in your household and what rules would be the most helpful for your child to learn given their age and ability. In addition, children who are hyperactive or who have poor attention need support in keeping simple rules. For example, it is very important that they only play with one toy at a time. Too many toys in the room at the same time only add to their distraction and reduce their attention. A simple rule that is important to keep is that they must tidy away a toy before moving onto a new activity.

Use 'Do's' rather than 'Don'ts'

One of the most common types of instructions parents give to children is a 'Don't' instruction. They say something like, 'Don't hit your sister' or 'Don't go near the TV'. However, 'Don't' commands are ineffective because they focus a child on the negative behaviour we don't want and tell him nothing about what we want to happen. If we say to a child, 'Don't go near the TV', this immediately focuses him on the TV and acts almost as a suggestion to go and play with it. The instruction might even make playing near the TV more attractive than before! In addition, the 'Don't' instruction tells him nothing about what he can do instead. With 'Don't' commands we give few ideas to children about how to behave correctly. Equally, we are more likely to give 'Don't' instructions angrily, and this sets up the expectation that the child is about to misbehave. For this reason, it is really important that you only give positive 'Do' instructions to children. All negatively framed commands can be made positive. All 'Don'ts' can be turned into 'Dos'.

- 'Don't grab the doll from your sister' can become, 'Please ask your sister to share the toys'.
- 'Don't shout in the house' can become, 'Please use a quiet voice in the house'.
- 'Don't hurt your little brother' can become, 'Please look after your little brother'.

Even if you catch yourself using a 'Don't', you can offer a 'Do' immediately afterwards. For example, if you say, 'Don't play with the TV', you can immediately follow up with a 'Do', such as, 'Come over and play with your Lego' or 'You can come over here; I'll help you draw.'

Get down to a child's level

A young child often doesn't understand what a parent has asked her to do. The parent may have used over-complicated language or may simply not have got the child's attention. It is best if you make your requests very clearly to your children. This means getting down to their level, ensuring you are face to face, that you make eye contact and have the child's full attention before you tell them what you want. With young children who are preoccupied with something else, this can mean kneeling down beside them and guiding them to look at you. In addition, you have to make sure to use very simple language that the children can understand and back it up with clear gestures. For example, when you want a child to put a block in the box, you can point at the block and then at the box, saying, 'Block in the box'.

Give children time

One of the biggest mistakes that parents make is that they don't give children time to comply with an instruction or to do what they ask. They bunch instructions together and may have given three or four before the child has had a chance to carry out the first one. This leaves the child confused and burdened and invariably leads to conflict. When you ask a child to do something, we suggest you wait at least five seconds before you issue another instruction or before taking disciplinary action. It can be helpful to count to five silently in your head. This helps to defuse the situation, and gives children time to decide how to comply.

Giving children notice and reminders are also helpful. For example, when children are engrossed in play before bedtime it can be helpful to remind them of bedtime by saying, 'You can play for ten more minutes and then it is bed time'. This gives children time to prepare and make choices about how to end their play.

Praise Cooperation

It is important to get into the habit of praising children when they cooperate with your rules. Commenting positively each time they do what you ask takes any 'power victory' out of the experience, and helps children see it as rewarding to be cooperative.

Often parents don't feel like thanking a child when they do something they are told, or they feel it is something the child should do anyway without praise. However, the problem with this approach is that unrewarded behaviour soon disappears. If parents wish to encourage their children's cooperation, thanking them when they do what they are told can make all the difference.

Remind children of what comes next

Reminding children of something more positive coming after an undesired task is a good way to get their cooperation. This is best exemplified by the 'When-Then Instruction':

> 'When you have put the blocks in the box, then you can take out the trucks.'

> 'When you calm down, then you will be able to visit Nana.'

The 'When-Then instruction' helps children cooperate because it lets them see the benefits and positive results of their actions. Over time it is a good way of teaching children discipline – doing difficult tasks first before having a reward.

'When-Then' provides you with a simple way of phrasing an instruction, and when combined with gestures and emphasis on the important words, even a young child with little language can understand it. In the first example above, you may clearly point to the blocks and then the box (and even guide the child's hand to put them away). The instruction can be further simplified to 'Blocks, then trucks.' Or in the second example, you might put your finger over your mouth and use a quiet voice saying, 'Ssh, then Nana's.'

TAKING THE LEAD DURING MISBEHAVIOUR

During misbehaviour or difficult situations, it can be useful to give a child a clear instruction about what you want to happen. Often a clear instruction or distraction is sufficient to get them back on track.

Assertively tell your child what you want

When a child misbehaves, parents can respond by assertively correcting the child and giving a simple instruction about what they can do instead.

- 'I don't like you pulling my hair; please keep your hands to yourself.'
- 'No, you can't play with Mammy's phone, but you can play with your blocks.'
- 'Don't use an angry voice with Daddy, use a nice voice.'

Sometimes a parent need not refer to the problem behaviour and simply tell the child what he would like to happen. For example, on seeing a child throw sand close to another child, the parent can say:

> 'Julie, (to get attention), please keep the sand in the box.'

Or in a supermarket, seeing a child starting to run, the parent can say:

> 'Please hold my hand while we are in the shop.'

To ensure that assertive corrections and instructions work well, it is important to make sure that you get the child's attention and make eye contact, and that you use a calm, but firm tone of voice. When you combine this with a matching facial expression you prevent a tense atmosphere from developing and you make it easier for your child to cooperate.

Distract your child with a new activity

With young children, distractions are excellent ways to lead away from misbehaviour. They work particularly well with very young children, who may not understand that misbehaviour is wrong or with children with special needs who find it harder to grasp consequences. The essential thing is to focus on what you want rather than what you don't want. Distractions are all about using 'Do' rather than 'Don't' instructions. Rather than saying 'Don't grab the sweets' to your child in the supermarket, which focuses his attention on the sweets, it can be more effective to distract him with a suggestion such as 'let's go and find the yoghurts you really like' which directs him to where you want to go.

> 'Let's play with the crayons now.'
> 'Oh, look what Mum has got for you here.'
> 'I have something special the two of you can do now... lets put away the toys and go outside.'

Once again, your tone of voice is crucial. An upbeat, positive tone of voice can focus even the most distracted child. In addition, distractions can be backed up with gestures or by gently guiding a child physically from a problem to a preferred activity.

> *Julie has a four-year-old boy Pete, who has a mild autistic spectrum disorder. Pete would often get into a screaming tantrum when something did not go his own way. Julie tried explaining and reasoning with Pete, but Pete would argue and shout back saying he hated his mum. When Julie tried to ignore Pete, his screams would escalate and sometimes he would become violent. Though Julie could sit out and ignore a tantrum, this was extremely upsetting for her and was not an option when they were in public (and this was the time that Pete was most likely to act up).*

Thinking about how best to respond, Julie came up with the following. She felt that ignoring Pete completely during a tantrum only made him worse (she thought this was related to Pete having autistic traits). Instead she found that it was better to try and soothe and listen to Pete while he was upset, (but not to give in to him) and then to distract him with a new activity. Though it was extremely hard, once she remained calm and in an upbeat way distracted Pete with something else to do, she discovered the strategy that worked best.

TIPS FOR GOING FORWARD

1 Think of the rules that are really important for your children to keep.

2 Write the rules down in terms of clear, polite assertive requests, for example, 'Please share with your sister' or 'Please tidy up now'.

3 Make sure to praise your children any time they keep the rules or do what you ask.

STEP 9

ASSERTIVE PARENTING

– FOLLOWING THROUGH ON RULES

I used to find it hard to be firm with my child. She would kick up a fuss and refuse to do what was asked, eventually (often after a long row) I would give in, and then feel bad about having done this. Things changed when I learned to respond in a much calmer and more assertive manner. I found that if I could keep my own tone of voice calm and be gently persistent, this was the best way to get my child to cooperate. When I was calm it was easier to be firm and I was less likely to give in. I also felt better that I had remained in control.

ASSERTIVELY FOLLOWING THROUGH ON RULES

Even when you give children clear, positive instruction and even when you set reasonable rules and limits, there will still be frequent times when children object and choose not to comply. It is normal, and indeed healthy, for children to test their parents' rules and limits. Parents must respond to this challenge and ensure children experience the consequences of such testing. What counts is that you know how to calmly follow through and insist on rules. This helps children learn to cooperate and understand the effects of their actions. The key is to be assertive – that is you remain calm and gently persistent as you take action to ensure that your child eventually cooperates. There are also a number of useful strategies that can help in giving children choices and enforcing consequences.

Use Choices and Consequences

A respectful and effective way to help children comply with instructions and rules is to use choices and consequences. Rather than trying to coerce or force children to do something, you offer them a choice between doing what you ask and a consequence for not doing so. The goal is to make it rewarding for them to take the choice you suggest and have an unrewarding consequence when they don't. The more reasonable and fair these consequences are, the more powerful the lesson is. When explaining a consequence to a child it is important to use a calm but firm tone of voice when giving the choice to the child. You want your child to take it seriously but you don't want them to experience it as a threat. Examples of effective choices and consequences are as follows:

> 'Either you tidy up now, or I'll take the toys away.'
> 'If you don't go to bed now, there won't be time for a story.'
> 'You can either play with the dollies or the teddies (and not the TV).'
> 'If you spill the milk then you have to clean it up.'

Other 'choices' can be given in the form of the 'When-Then instruction':

'When you tidy away the blocks, then you can play with the cars.'
'When you put your coat on, then you can go outside.'

The child has a choice as to how to respond. If he chooses to put his coat on then he can go outside, and if he chooses not to, he stays in. Choices work because they give the power back to children and let them decide how to respond. In the long term, such an approach helps him learn to take responsibility for his actions. Consequences are an excellent way to teach children how to behave and are much better than nagging or criticising, which give a child a lot of negative attention for misbehaving (and thus often makes the misbehaviour much worse).

Even children as young as two can understand choices and consequences, but it is important to frame them in simple language and back up your words with clear gestures and body language. For example, *'Blocks* in the *box*, then *cars'* or 'Eat your *peas*, then *ice cream'* (pointing at each of the objects as they are said).

ENFORCING CONSEQUENCES

If you do use choices, you must be prepared to enforce them – you must let the children experience the consequences of their choices. For example, if you have set the rule of only playing with one toy at a time, and if the child does not tidy the blocks up, you must insist he does not move on to play with the cars.

1   It is best to enforce consequences calmly and firmly in a relaxed way. Don't make it into a power struggle. Be gentle and insistent. Don't think you are winning one over on your

child, simply see it as teaching them how to behave better and helping them learn how to be responsible.

2 Simply say what you are doing, 'No more Lego now, because you threw it at Joe.' But don't get into long explanations or arguments. Remember enforcing a consequence is a time for action and not words.

3 Where possible give your child some control. For example, when taking a toy from a child, put your hand out for him to choose to give it to you, before you might take it from him. This is much more respectful and dignified.

4 When enforcing consequences it is a good idea to ignore a child's protests and whines. Simply let them pass you by and don't get drawn into an argument. Calmly and firmly follow through.

5 Once you have enforced the consequence, you can consider talking with your child about the rule and the reasons for it. Generally, it is a good idea to do this at another time, away from the heat of the conflict when the child is likely to be calmer.

ENFORCING CHOICES AND CONSEQUENCES – AN EXAMPLE

1 Child spotted misbehaving (for example, drawing on the table).

2 Parent gives instruction, 'Lucy you must draw on the paper and keep the table nice and clean.'

3 Parent shows child how to do it, 'Look we draw like this' (hand over hand).

4 Child continues to draw on table.

5 Parent gives choice, 'Draw on paper or no drawing'.

6 Child continues to draw on the table.

7 Parent takes the crayons away.

8 Parent describes their own actions, 'We have to put the crayons away now because you drew on the table' (in a calm, matter of fact voice, ignoring all protests).
9 Parent gets child to help clean up, 'Now we must clean up the mess'.
10 Parent moves on cheerfully to next activity without referring to misbehaviour.

> *Using choices with my four-year-old daughter worked like magic for me. She was the type of child who hated to be told what to do; she hated anyone ordering her. Giving her choices about what to do next helped her hold onto some of the control and retain her dignity. For example, instead of arguing with her over eating vegetables at dinner, I'd say, 'What vegetable would you like for dinner? You can have broccoli or carrots'. Or instead of getting into a fight at bedtime, I'd say, 'I'll read you a story when you are sitting in the bed – it is your choice'. Of course, it meant that I had to plan ahead and think through what choices I could give her in potentially conflictual situations but it still worked well.*

TIME OUT – A SPECIAL CONSEQUENCE

If a child misbehaves in a way which you can't ignore (for example, hitting someone, or getting over-angry) and for which there is no natural consequence, you can use a procedure called 'Time Out' to manage the situation. 'Time Out' is essentially insisting a child sits in a 'naughty chair' or sending them to another room for a short period to help them calm down. The aim of 'Time Out' is not so much to punish a child, but more to interrupt a negative behaviour and to help a child learn to calm down.

'Time Out' should not be used excessively and it is not a replacement for positive parenting such as encouragement and rewards. The positive aspects of parenting are the things that make the difference in teaching children how to behave well in the long term. However, 'Time Out' does provide a way of managing difficult behaviour that teaches responsibility and is less damaging than alternative reactions such as shouting at a child, or threatening physical discipline.

DON'T WORRY—
JUST BECAUSE IT'S
A 'TIME OUT'
DOESN'T MEAN YOU
ACTUALLY HAVE TO
GO OUT!

What age child can I use 'Time Out' with?

For 'Time Out' to work, children have to understand that it is related to a specific type of behaviour, such as hitting. In addition, they need to understand that 'Time Out' is for a short period of time and only until they are calm or prepared to say sorry. You need to make sure they are not frightened by the prospect of 'Time Out' and don't see it as your loss of love for them. Your child needs to be old enough to understand these things before you can use this approach (usually at least three-years-old depending on the child's ability). For this reason we suggest you explain 'Time Out' in advance to your children so you can make sure they understand.

Explaining 'Time Out' in advance

It is important to sit down with children in advance (and during a conflict situation) to explain 'Time Out' to them. It is important to be positive about the purpose. You might explain that it is about helping them to get on better together or learning better ways of resolving disagreements other than hitting out. Explain that it is about helping everyone – children and parents – to calm down in tense situations, and avoid rows and shouting which might otherwise occur. There are a number of key points that need to be covered in the explanation:

Which behaviour?
Children need to be absolutely clear which behaviour will lead to 'Time Out' (hitting out, or breaking things). Parents should stick to this and not include other types of behaviour in the heat of the moment.

Where?
Children should know where 'Time Out' will take place. This ideally should be a safe place where there are not too many distractions. A hallway or bedroom is often used. For younger children, a chair facing the corner can be sufficient, though it may be necessary to have a back-up room if the child refuses to stay in the chair. The 'Time Out' location should not be a scary or unsafe place such as a shed or a bathroom where medicines are kept. If you feel the child is likely to be distressed by going to the 'Time Out' room you may wish to show him exactly where he will have to go in advance, reassuring him that it is simply a way of helping him to behave better.

How long?
'Time Out' only needs to be short (about five minutes) to be effective. It should not be longer than ten minutes unless the

child continues to make a fuss. The essential rule is that children need to be quiet for at least two minutes before they can come out. This means that if they protest, shout or scream, they will have to stay there longer. The goal of 'Time Out' is to interrupt negative behaviour and to help children learn self-control and how to calm down. If they are let out while they are protesting or still angry, this defeats the purpose.

Explain using pictures

A picture sequence is an excellent way to explain 'Time Out' to a young child who may have little verbal language. In the pictures attached the process is divided into very simple steps. (See **Figure 9.1,** p.110)

With young children the pictures are best redrawn and made personal to your child using their name and the exact situation. (Remember it is not a test of your art!) In addition, it is a good idea to include just one picture per page and to show the pictures to your child as if you were reading a storybook. The essential thing in the explanation is to show the child the positive ending to the 'Time Out' – he can come out to play and Jamie and Mummy are happy.

An *example of 'Time Out'* Step by Step

1 Child engages in bad behaviour for which there is no natural consequence (for example, bites his brother).
2 Parent consoles injured brother, giving lots of attention.
3 Parent moves child to 'Time Out', 'You bit your brother; he's hurt and I am cross, now you go to "Time Out".' (Note the parents gives a brief explanation. With less serious situations, it could be appropriate to give a warning, 'If you throw the toy again, you will have to go to "Time Out"').
4 Child brought to 'Time Out' chair (ignore protests), 'You can come out when you are ready to play like friends'.

5   Parent continues to attend to injured brother.

6   If child leaves chair, he is brought firmly back with no discussion.

7   If child leaves again, he is put outside the door ('Now you have to do "Time Out" in the hall').

8   After two minutes, or as soon as child is calm or shows genuine remorse he is allowed back in.

9   Parent can name feelings, to help child understand, 'I know your brother sometimes takes your toys but you can't bite him…'

10 Child may be guided in how to apologise or make amends ('Now say sorry to your brother').

TIPS FOR GOING FORWARD

1   Identify a rule you want to ensure your child keeps during the coming week.

2   Think up a plan as to how you will calmly and assertively ensure that your child keeps the rule.

3   Think up choices and consequences that you can use to help your child learn to keep the rule.

Figure 9.1

Parents Plus 2003

Time Out

Page 1

If Jim hits   Jim sits down

Page 2

When Jim's quiet   We'll be friends

Page 3

Mummy's happy   Jim's happy

STEP 10

USING REWARDS TO TEACH CHILDREN TO BEHAVE WELL

My three-year-old son wouldn't eat dinner in the evenings. The more I would tell or remind him the more he would resist. One thing that helped was using pictures and a reward chart. I drew up a chart with seven dinner plates on it and explained to him that each evening that he ate his dinner he would be allowed colour in one of the plates and when they were all coloured in we could go out for a trip to the playground at the weekend. I chose colouring in because this was something he loved to do and I think this made him very interested. I think also because he was colouring in dinner plates this kept him focused on what he had to do.

Solving behavioural problems is often about teaching children a task or skill that they haven't yet mastered, whether this is learning to share with other children or learning to sit at the table during breakfast. As well as using praise and encouragement, rewards can be very effective in helping children learn – providing them with a special motivation to succeed. However, to make rewards work, you have to follow a number of principles.

MAKING REWARDS EFFECTIVE

Be clear about the behaviour you want

When using rewards some parents are vague about what behaviour they are trying to teach, for example, giving a child a treat for 'being good'. Also, sometimes parents reward the absence of a negative behaviour they don't want, for example, 'not fighting' or 'not staying up late'. The trouble with these approaches is that they don't tell your child exactly what you want and in the latter example they highlight the behaviour you don't want. For this reason it is important to be very clear and positive about the behaviour you do want and to make sure the child understands clearly what he has to do to get the reward.

Use motivating rewards

It is important to use rewards which are of great interest to your child, and which they will work hard for. This varies from child to child and depends very much on your child's age. Rewards don't have to be expensive to be effective. Even older children can be motivated by ordinary treats like extra playtime or a special trip. It is important to put some time into thinking which rewards will work for your child. It often helps to ask the child what he or she would like (within limits) as a reward, as this will really make him motivated to succeed. Examples of good rewards are:

- staying up later.
- special time with parents in the evening.
- an extra bedtime story.
- going shopping with a parent.
- a trip out to the park or playground.
- taking out a special toy that is not used frequently (the paddling pool in the garden).
- a bubble bath.

Reward Charts

Reward charts are an excellent way to motivate children. Some younger children may be rewarded enough by simply colouring or pasting a token or sticker onto the reward chart for each instance of good behaviour. Other children will need to have an extra special treat once enough tokens are collected.

In designing a chart, be creative. Think about what motivates and interests your child and try to incorporate this into the chart. If your child likes flowers, you make a reward chart with a picture of a garden with lots of flower stems with the tops missing. Each time your child behaves well she can draw a flower top. Similarly if your child likes trains you could draw a big picture of a train engine on tracks. Then each time she behaves well, she can colour a carriage on the train. When all the carriages are full, then she gets to go on a trip on the train.

Making reward charts work for young children

- The more colourful and attractive the chart is the more appealing it will be. Equally the bigger the better (children love a big chart about them on a wall).

- The chart should incorporate a picture related to the targeted good behaviour on the chart as well as the reward if possible. A photo of your child sleeping is an excellent addition to a bedtime chart – keeping her focused on what you want her to do.

- Draw the chart with your child and act out the behaviour to help your child understand the sequence. Sticking relevant photos on the chart may also help the young child relate the chart to the good behaviour. For example, taking a photo of a child on the toilet and putting it at the top of the sticker chart on the bathroom wall.

- Use simple language to describe each picture on the chart. This is especially important for young children or children with little language – you want to make sure they understand the connection between their good behaviour and the reward.

- Once earned, keep the stars on the chart – don't take them away for misbehaviour.

It is a good idea to collect completed reward charts in a scrapbook so that you can look back at these together and keep your child motivated.

Reward chart examples

At the end of this section we have several examples of reward charts as follows:

1 *Using the Toilet:*
   If a child uses the toilet he could be rewarded by putting a sticker on a large picture of a toilet on the wall.

2 *Eating Breakfast:*
   If a child eats up all his breakfast he gets to colour a bowl and spoon a different colour each time.

3 *Going Shopping:*

If a child stays beside Mum and Dad when at the shop each morning, he gets to colour a step up the top of the hill. When all the steps are coloured in, he gets to go on a special trip to the park.

4 *Eating Dinner:*

If a child stays sitting on the chair during dinner she draws a happy face on the chart. Once she has earned eight smiling faces she can be rewarded with a video.

Example 1 – Using the Toilet

Parents Plus 2003

Example 2 – Eating Breakfast

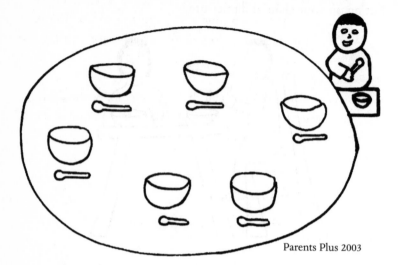

Parents Plus 2003

Example 3 – Going Shopping

Staying with Mum at the shops

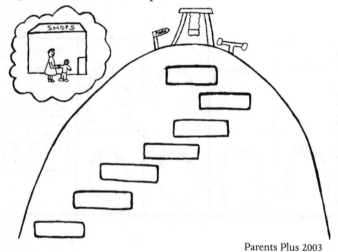

Parents Plus 2003

Example 4 – Eating Dinner

Sitting on your chair at dinner time

Parents Plus 2003

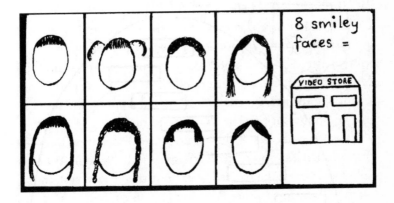

8 smiley faces =

VIDEO STORE

Start small

One of the reasons reward systems can sometimes fail is that they may initially be too difficult for the child, and when he fails to get the reward on the first few attempts he gives up, feeling disappointed. So it is important to start small, with behaviour that is easy enough for him to achieve. In the example of the bedtime chart, the process is broken down into small steps each of which he could achieve and be rewarded for:

- Two stars at night if he washes and puts pyjamas on.
- Two extra stars in the morning if he stays in bed and goes to sleep.

The system can be made even clearer by colour coding night and morning stars to help the child know exactly what is needed (for instance, use silver stars for getting ready for bed, but special gold stars for going to sleep and staying in bed all night).

Use lots of encouragement

Rewards aren't a replacement for verbal encouragement and approval. In fact, they work best if they are backed up by lots of positive attention and kind words. As you reward your child using the chart, each time remind them clearly why they are getting the reward, for example, 'You did a poo in the toilet so now you put a stick on the chart. Good boy.'

Rewards work best if they are not used excessively, but only for special occasions or to learn specific behaviour. When a child has learned the desired behaviour the reward system can be phased out over time. For example, when a child gets into the habit of going to bed on time, a mother can phase out the bedtime star system, replacing it with ordinary positive attention. If the child is still motivated to gain stars, a new desired type of behaviour can be selected such as sitting at the table or getting dressed quickly

Tips for Going Forward

1 Make a list of the rewards that you know will really motivate your child.
2 Think of a new behaviour you want to teach her.
3 Do up a reward chart with your child that will help motivate her to learn the new behaviour.
4 Make sure to involve her in the making of the chart and the choice of the reward.

Also by the Authors

Sharry, J. *Bringing up Responsible Children* (Dublin: Veritas, 1999)

Sharry, J. *Bringing up Responsible Teenagers* (Dublin: Veritas 2001)

Sharry, J. *Solution Focused Groupwork* (London: Sage, 2001)

Sharry, J., Reid, P., & Donohoe, E. *When parents separate: A guide to helping you and your children cope* (Dublin: Veritas, 2001)

Sharry, J., Madden, B., & Darmody, M. *Becoming a solution-focused detective: A strengths-based guide to brief therapy* (London: Brief Therapy Press, 2001)

Sharry, J. *Parent Power: Bringing up responsible children and teenagers* (Chichester: Wiley, 2002)

Fitzpatrick, C., Sharry, J. *Coping with Depression in Young People: A Guide for Parents* (Chichester: Wiley, 2004)

Sharry, J. *Counselling children, adolescents and families: A strengths-based collaborative approach* (London: Sage, 2004)

CLINICAL INTERVENTION PROGRAMMES

Sharry, J., & Fitzpatrick, C. (2001). *Parents Plus Families and Adolescents Programme: A video-based guide to managing conflict and getting on better with older children and teenagers aged 11-16: www.parentsplus.ie*

Sharry, J., Hampson, G., & Fanning, M. (2003). *Parents Plus - 'The Early Years' Programme: A video-based parenting guide to promoting young children's development and to preventing and managing behaviour problems. www.parentsplus.ie*